The Children's Kitchen Garden

The Children's Kitchen Garden

A Book of Gardening, Cooking, and Learning

Georgeanne and Ethel Brennan

with Marcel Barchechat
and the East Bay French-American School

Illustrations by Ann Arnold

Ten Speed Press
Berkeley, California

🔁

Ten Speed Press
P.O. Box 7123
Berkeley, California 94707

Distributed in Australia by Simon & Schuster Australia, in Canada by Publishers Group West, in New Zealand by Tandem Press, in South Africa by Real Books, in the United Kingdom and Europe by Airlift Books, and in Singapore and Malaysia by Berkeley Books.

Cover and interior design by Catherine Jacobes
Cover and interior illustrations by Ann Arnold
Photography by April Gertler
Puff Pastry–Topped Ratatouille by Lorena Jones
Vegetable Pockets by Heather Garnos

Library of Congress Cataloging-in-Publication Data
Brennan, Georgeanne, 1943-
    The children's kitchen garden; a book of gardening, cooking, and learning / Georgeanne and Ethel Brennan with Marcel Barchechat and the East Bay French–American School.
        p.   cm.
    Includes bibliographical refernces (p.   ) and index.
ISBN 0-89815-873-7
    1. Children's gardens.   2. Vegetable gardening.   3. Gardening-
-Experiments.   4.Botany--Experiments.   5. Botany--Study and
teaching--Activity programs.   6. East Bay French-American School
(Berkeley, Calif.)   7. School gardens.   I. Brennan, Ethel.
II. Barchechat, Marcel.   III. East Bay French-American School
(Berkeley, Calif.)   IV. Title
SB457.B66   1997   96-52023
372.3'57--dc21   CIP

First printing, 1997
Printed in Hong Kong

2 3 4 5 6 - 00 99 98

Contents

I'm delighted that the kids have been given a garden project. It's so important that children are permitted—indeed, encouraged—to get wet, dirty, and buggy while exploring the source of real food. Whether they're collecting seeds beneath a sprout blossom or lifting carrots and radishes from the earth, they're weaving a relationship with the fundamentals of life.

—Viki von Lockum, farm manager,
Kona Kai Organic Farm

Thanks to the following children who appear in photographs throughout the book: Chloe Bean, Clara Brill, Gerald Cartaud, Maeve Clifford, Chloe Courchesne, Olivia DeLancie, Mari Diabankouezi, Melanie Ferre, Benjamin Hunt, Miles Kodama, Sophia Levis, Elizabeth McAlpine-Bellis, Alexandra McCoy, Filomene Morrison, Caroline Orsini, Jay Ross, Alexandra Ryan-Gutentag, Annie Sept, Rosie Shoemaker, Taryn Skubic, Nora Somogyi, Ian Stark, Griffin Stead-Kamer, Joshua Tan, and Vanessa Triplett.

Acknowledgments

THIS BOOK COULD not have come into being without the help, dedication, and participation of many, many people. The students, parents, and staff of the East Bay French-American School, Michael Norton and the crew at Kona Kai Organic Farm, the staff of Ten Speed Press, Green Gulch Farm, and the organic farmers, market growers, and their advocates who have worked so diligently to promote an understanding of sustainable agriculture and its rewards all have a place in these pages.

Without Lauren Webb, whose idea it was, this book could not have come to fruition. In the dual role as involved parent at the East Bay French-American School and part of the publishing group at Ten Speed Press, she had a vision of a book that would express her passion for teaching children about the importance of connecting with the earth and working with nature to support all living things. Lauren wanted a book that would demonstrate in both words and pictures the extraordinary feeling of wonder and understanding that comes when children grow and prepare their own food. She proposed the idea to the school and Ten Speed Press, and then as the process of writing, photographing, and illustrating began, Lauren remained at the center of the project, maintaining its integrity and lending every support from tending tomato plants to hand-holding authors and artists. Through the process of editing and design, Lauren's steady work kept the book on course. Thank you, Lauren, from everyone.

Denise Moullé's role has been pivotal throughout the project. Denise, also a parent at the East Bay French-American School, was wildly enthusiastic from the project's inception. She had been thinking about how one might introduce the French ideas about taste, food, and gardening to American children. An alliance was formed between Lauren and Denise. Denise worked with the headmaster and the Board of Directors at the school, found the authors and illustrator, and with Lauren made sure that the book never lost its original vision.

Ann Arnold put an extraordinary amount of time, thought, and effort into creating the playful and whimsical illustrations that grace these pages. She could often be seen sitting in the school's garden throughout the seasons, sketching and observing. Her sensibility and delight in the garden are evident on every page.

April Gertler, the photographer, walked the garden with the children, listening and watching them in order to capture their expressions as they dug into the dirt, pulled weeds, planted, and harvested their garden. She could be found there early in the morning and late in the afternoon, looking through her lens for the perfect moment.

So many people helped and we are especially grateful to the following: Edith Bourret-Courchesne, Gerald Cartaud, Philippe Dietz, Nathalie Donchery-Tovar, Thierry Durandard, Heather Garnos, April Gertler, Helene Jimenez, Wendy Johnson, Lorena Jones, Sandra Kerrest, Charlotte Kimball, Susan Lescher, Susan Maino, Kirsty Melville, Jean-Pierre Moullé, Tom Olson, Simone Pierce, Javier Quintero, Roberte Rountree, Jim Schrupp, Sharon Silva, and Viki von Lockum.

Introduction

IN 1994, THE EAST BAY French-American School, in Berkeley, California, started a garden project that has become an integral part of the school's curriculum and a source of pride for the students, faculty, and parents. The inspiration for this book about kitchen gardening for children comes from the dedicated and enthusiastic parents at the school who feel that their children's experiences with the garden project, and what their children are learning and accomplishing in the world of gardening, food, and taste, can be achieved at home and in other schools, even if the parents or teachers are not skilled gardeners.

Across the United States, there is an increased awareness of the need to teach children about their relationship to the land, and the importance of passing on this information to future generations. This understanding parallels an increased concern about the quality of the food we eat. A children's kitchen garden is a good beginning.

A well-tended kitchen garden allows children to experience daily the relationship between the earth and the food they eat. As they bring freshly dug carrots into the kitchen, the dirt still clinging to the spindle-shaped roots, children are spellbound by the notion that these beautiful vegetables were once tiny seeds, sown by their own hands weeks and weeks ago into the welcoming soil they themselves had prepared. They cared for those carrots and watched as the fluffy green tops formed above the ground, while their subterranean bounty developed below.

Once in the kitchen, children treat their harvest with awe and respect. It is a singular moment when they realize they have grown something from seed, pulled it from the soil, prepared it, and then eaten it. Whether simply steamed or buttered, grated into a salad, or part of a stew, the carrots and the children have a shared history that connects the children with nature and helps them to understand their role in the life cycle. In a kitchen garden, young gardeners develop a caretaking relationship with the earth and with their own bodies, while nurturing their garden in the simplest organic way, with compost and manure. They learn the importance of keeping their environment healthy, and consequently their own bodies.

The children's connection with the earth develops as they spend time in the garden, their hands thrust deep into the soil. Worms crawl and wiggle past, bugs dig, roots spread, and rocks and pebbles pierce the layers, all waiting to be discovered by reaching fingers. The power of the earth, sun, and water to bring forth and sustain life becomes apparent once the soil is prepared, the seeds planted, and the seedlings start to grow.

Gardening, cooking, and eating engage all the senses of even the youngest children. The unforgettable smell and feel of warm moist earth, the spicy aroma left behind on the hand after planting dill seeds, the perfume of silky young basil leaves, and even the sweet, musky scent of decaying melons can all be discovered in the garden. Carried to the kitchen, the earth's bounty continues to incite the senses. The snap and crunch of green beans and cucumbers signal their freshness. Firm yet ripe tomatoes release flavorful juices as they are sliced into perfect rounds. Bundles of cilantro and tarragon fill the room with their fragrance as they are snipped into a mound of aromatic shards.

The majority of young Americans do not grow up with gardening as a part of daily life, yet a garden is an ideal place to learn about the environment, the process by which seeds become food, and the importance of growing food in a sustainable, healthful fashion. We hope that this book will inspire parents, grandparents, teachers, and other caregivers to embark upon a joyful and instructive gardening experience with children that will give them a profound knowledge of taste, cooking, and food.

In France, fresh, seasonal vegetables, herbs, and fruits are considered a birthright. From the earliest age, children are taught not just to eat their food, but to savor the flavors. Infants are fed carefully seasoned purées of newly harvested carrots with a hint of dill, artichoke hearts simmered in chicken broth, and green beans cooked with fresh thyme. From the time they are toddlers, French children are helped to plant a little garden of radishes and lettuce. They are accompanied as they inspect the growing plants and, when their produce is ready, they are encouraged to brush off the dirt from a freshly pulled radish and to eat it while standing in the garden. Then they proudly bring the rest of their harvest into the kitchen, to share with all the family. As a child learns to walk and to talk, to draw, to paint, and to play, so does he or she learn about food, its flavors and aromas, its origins and its uses. Most often, this instruction occurs in the family, imparted by a parent, a relative, or a close friend, but the notion of developing taste and the other senses has been institutionalized in the French schoolroom as well.

The curriculum of the French national school system has progressive units on taste and food beginning at the preschool level and continuing through the fifth grade. The program demonstrates the biological mechanism of seed germination, seedling emergence, and the plant's growth cycle for fruits and vegetables, and then explains the relationship of the cycle to seasonality and to the food we eat. For example, a discussion of spinach is taken from the sowing of the seed, through germination and growth, to its conclusion in the kitchen, where it is transformed into the familiar *épinards au gratin* (spinach gratin). The study of food is also linked to the study of geography, so that children are taught to identify apples with Normandy, oysters with Brittany, and wheat with the Île-de-France.

At the French-American School, headmaster Marcel Barchechat passionately believes that children who actively participate in their own education shape their lives in profound ways. This small school

of five hundred students, from preschool through eighth grade, has taken the French respect for food and the nation's curriculum on taste and food a step further by creating a school garden where the students sow seeds, transplant seedlings, inspect insects, and maintain their plants; taste and evaluate the vegetables as they grow; and finally, cook from their garden. In this multidisciplinary setting, classroom science lessons take on a practical reality. Writing and note taking are more than mere exercises, and nutritional information becomes personal. Growing a vegetable from start to finish and then preparing it, directly from the garden, produces an intense sense of achievement and pride. Food is a basic need and it is a thrilling moment for children when they realize that it is possible to provide good-tasting food from their own labor. It is no less thrilling to understand that food, its preparation and its sharing, is an immensely pleasurable social extension of that basic need.

The same exhilaration born out of discovery and out of the exploration of the world of the senses experienced by the children at the French-American School can happen in nearly any American home or school. A huge garden space isn't required. As long as there is adequate sun and water, growing, tasting, and cooking with vegetables and fruits in season can be accomplished with a garden no larger than a planter box, a large pot, or half a barrel on a porch or balcony.

The importance and pleasure of tending a garden with children and watching its transformation, even if it is no more than a wooden crate of green onions or a tub of Mediterranean herbs, take precedence here over elaborate planting schemes and complex methodology. So, too, does the notion that bringing the garden, the table, and the home together is the end desire of having a vegetable garden.

We have organized the book into six chapters. Chapter 1 gives the background of the East Bay French-American School garden project, with examples of garden and classroom activities. Chapter 2 provides a narrative for organizing a similar educational experience in a home or school garden. Chapter 3 presents the practical how-to, hands-on information needed to start and maintain a garden for teaching children, and contains an annotated listing of eighteen edible plants. The listings not only include directions for growing, but also what to look for as the crops reach maturity and are ready to harvest, so that even parents or teachers with little or no horticultural knowledge can be informed guides throughout the gardening process. There are also suggestions for simple ways to prepare the harvest for the table. Chapter 4 gives profiles for thirteen different herbs, suggests two easy herb garden plans, and offers nine simple herb-based recipes. Chapter 5 introduces four seasonal gardens, with recipes accompanying each one. Chapter 6 has special cooking tips for children, plus more easy and delicious recipes using garden produce.

Dispersed throughout the book are garden, science, tasting, and cooking activities for adults and children, as well as over thirty recipes that include tasks in which even small children can participate.

THE IDEA FOR A GARDEN

THE IDEA FOR A GARDEN planted and maintained by Ecole Bilingue students came from my observation that children raised in the United States differ from their French counterparts in their knowledge about food sources and taste differentiation. I hoped to expose the students here to foods other than the hamburgers and hot dogs that were so prevalent in their everyday lives. I thought that the garden in a bilingual school would provide a way for the children to learn French in a more stimulating environment than what the typical classroom offered. The plan was for them to be able to sow the seeds, watch the plants grow, pick the fruits or vegetables, and eat them.

It is very important that children growing up in an urban environment be exposed to garden experiences if society is to improve its way of living. Children with access to a garden early in life will find the experiences learned in it natural rather than strange.

One class at the Ecole Bilingue planted the ingredients for making a salad in the school garden. Later, they picked the vegetables and actually prepared a salad. When they sat down to enjoy what they had created, the teacher suggested that they not rush, but that they savor the dish, as it was the result of their own efforts. This is an important alternative to "eating and running," which is more common for our students.

And so, Ecole Bilingue has successfully created a hands-on gardening experience for its students. This has enabled the teachers to incorporate botanical concepts into our science curriculum through real-life experiences. It has also begun to change our students' perceptions and habits regarding food and its consumption.

—MARCEL BARCHECHAT, HEADMASTER OF THE
EAST BAY FRENCH-AMERICAN SCHOOl

CHAPTER ONE

The French-American Approach

THE PRIVATE EAST BAY French-American School, or L'Ecole Bilingue, was founded in 1977, in Berkeley, California, by a small group of parents who wanted a bicultural French and English school for their children. Its goal was to provide children of families from varying social and economic backgrounds with a high-quality academic education in a culturally diverse environment.

A board of trustees, composed primarily of parents, administers the school, manages the finances, and oversees school policies. Originally the school had about fifty students in grades kindergarten through third, but by 1997 it had grown to include preschool through eighth grade and some five hundred students. The parents, as primary caregivers and educators, use the school to continue the educational development of their children in a manner that reflects their own beliefs and values. This occurs through a curriculum that combines the educational practices and philosophies of both the French and the American school systems, resulting in a setting that requires high academic standards while encouraging creativity and self-development.

Specifically, the curriculum of the Ecole Bilingue incorporates aspects of the educational system of the Education Nationale de France and the California State Framework for Public Schools. In France, the government, through the Ministère de l'Education Nationale, determines the standards to be followed by all French public schools, from kindergarten through twelfth grade. Students in France are taught in a structured environment, and academic discipline and strong work habits characterize the French educational system.

The French Ecole Maternelle, which encompasses the preschool and kindergarten years, is a respected institution used as a model throughout the world. French children can enter school at two years of age to learn social skills while their physical and cognitive development is fostered in a caring environment. The system becomes increasingly academic in first grade and throughout elementary school, where children receive intensive instruction in reading, writing, and mathematics. Typically an elementary school day begins at 8:30 and lasts until 4:30 in the afternoon. Mornings center around academic subjects, followed by a two-hour break during which children can go home for lunch and relaxation. The afternoon may include more academic subjects but is usually dedicated to less involved subjects, such as art, music, social studies, and physical education.

Unlike in France, the public school system in the United States is administered by the individual states, rather than the federal government. Control may be further decentralized by state governments at their discretion, delegating power to county and local governments and to individual schools. In California, the state has developed the California State Framework for Public Schools, a general curriculum guideline for kindergarten through the twelfth grade, the implementation of which is the responsibility of local authorities.

Public education in the United States takes an active role in the health, socialization, and citizenship of children at all grade levels, and the development of the whole person is considered in concert with academic training, an approach that allows for a more individualized and creative teaching style than that of the French system. For example, creative learning in math is practiced through the use of models and exercises from which children learn formulas and facts through experience, trial and error, and discovery. This method enables students to learn at their own pace, especially in the early years.

Another significant difference between the two educational approaches is the role parents play in the schools. American parents are expected and encouraged to participate with their children's teachers and in school activities, as volunteers in classrooms, as after-school assistants, and as members of Parent-Teacher Associations. In France, the classroom is the domain of the teacher, although parents can participate in the schools through the Parents' Associations and the School Councils established in every French school.

Because the Ecole Bilingue has devised a style of schooling that combines demanding academic expectations, creative approaches to teaching, and parental involvement in all aspects of a child's education, the students are rewarded with a strong sense of scholastic achievement accomplished through rigorous and systematic lessons and a wide variety of imaginative activities. The school's garden project is an example of a program that marries a creative learning model with structured lesson plans to educate children in a multidisciplinary way.

The genesis of the garden project may be found in several sources: the pedagogical beliefs and experiences of the school's headmaster, Marcel Barchechat; the influence of Jacques Puisais's work with children in France; and the parents' desire for their children to develop an understanding of how food is grown, how it tastes, how it is cooked, and how growing food relates to the health of the environment and their own bodies.

Headmaster since 1989, Barchechat has long shared the value that French society places on food, and thinks that to understand where food comes from and how it connects people together within society is an integral part of learning. As an educator, he felt a need to provide such instruction for his pupils, using a garden as a vehicle for learning.

Upon reading *Le Goût et L'Enfant (Taste and the Child)*, by Jacques Puisais and Catherine Pierre, Barchechat was further convinced of the importance of teaching about food and taste and of the validity of having a school garden. Puisais, a noted French enologist, views food as a primary means for developing all the senses, and in the early 1970s, in the fifth-grade classrooms at Tours, he began a series of classes to "awaken the senses." In *Le Goût et L'Enfant*, he recounts the philosophy behind the program and provides detailed lessons and activities.

Tastings

Food tastings are an important part of the Ecole Bilingue's gardening program, and many foods, even ones not grown in the garden, are used to teach the students about taste. The purpose of such an exercise is to engage the children in an activity that will help them to develop a sense of taste that they will carry through life. The gathering might focus on cheeses, stone fruits, chocolates, breads, olives, or herbs.

The process can be as simple as having the children dip bread into small dishes of vegetable oils, such as olive, peanut, corn, sesame, and palm, and then encouraging them to discuss the different oils. At home, this tasting exercise can be taken a step further by making two batches of muffins, one with olive oil and one with a light corn oil, and then talking about the taste, texture, and appearance of both batches. Extending the tasting to a cooking exercise will show children how their new knowledge about food and taste translates into meal preparation.

Puisais's classes were designed to teach children about taste through sight, smell, and touch, in addition to the actual tasting of food. The four base flavors, sweet, sour, bitter, and salty, were studied in depth, and the students learned to identify them in prepared dishes. They also cooked with Puisais, creating meals using their newly acquired food knowledge. How an individual's taste is developed over time, influenced by surroundings and personal experience, and how the act of tasting involves not only the taste buds, but also smell and sight, were also explored. For example, a fresh green bean picked from the vine is firm and smooth to the touch, suggesting a sweet, crisp taste, and visually has a bright, inviting color. An old green bean is limp to the touch, slightly brown, and may have an unappetizing sour smell.

Encouraged by the work of Puisais, Barchechat felt that a similar program, especially in the context of the long-dreamed-of school garden, would be enjoyed by the school's students, and would also provide them with invaluable knowledge to carry with them throughout life. Translated excerpts from Puisais's *Le Goût et L'Enfant* are found throughout this book.

Taste

The essential question of the diversity of taste between individuals remains. All humans are not born equal in terms of gustatory perception—quite simply because every person's sensory system is unique. Each individual has several hundred chemical receptors [located] under his tongue. According to Annick Faurion, a specialist on the subject, these receptors vary both in number and in type, which explains the differences in responses to taste tests. Just as there are color-blind people, there are people who are "taste blind."

Color

The color of food supplies [us with] information about its authenticity, its freshness, its degree of maturity and—when dealing with cooked food—its "doneness." Children should be taught early to gather the information that color provides.

—From *Le Goût et L'Enfant (Taste and the Child)*
by Jacques Puisais

In 1994, a school garden program was initiated, driven by the goals of learning to garden, to explore the senses, and to cook, all in relation to the environment. In effect, a French kitchen garden *(potager)* was established, where students could learn the practicalities of technical gardening and explore the world of taste.

Traditionally, a *potager* supplies the French kitchen with fresh vegetables and herbs throughout the year. The garden typically includes seasonal vegetables and often has a few fruit trees on its boundaries or at its center. Each season has its stars. In spring, the *potager* boasts tender, young lettuces and spinach, plump fava beans, the first carrots, shoots of green onions and green garlic, and early radishes and peas. Handfuls of springtime herbs—chervil, tarragon, parsley, chives, dandelion—flavor the daily repasts, and strawberries, cherries, and apricots are folded into desserts. When summer arrives, the *potager* supplies the cook with crunchy *haricots verts* (snap beans), juicy tomatoes, glistening purple eggplants, and a bountiful harvest of summer squashes. Basil, thyme, sage, and rosemary provide the herbal accents of the season, while peaches, nectarines, plums, melons, berries, and figs fill the fruit bowl. In fall, the *potager* harvest brings colorful hard-skinned winter squashes, meaty shelling beans, and fresh potatoes. The cool-season lettuces, frisée, radishes, carrots, and spinach that first appeared in spring are once again in the garden. Fall apples, pears, and quinces are gathered, some to be stored away. Even in winter,

Next the fruits are cut in half, and the children are asked to note the differences in the thicknesses of the rinds.

Finally, the fruits are juiced and they are sampled one at a time, so that the tastes can be compared. The students tell the director what differences they notice. Although they sometimes have difficulty finding the words to describe their observations, they are nonetheless enthusiastic and willing.

the *potager* supplies the kitchen with fresh vegetables. Cabbage, leeks, kale, and parsnips are common fare, and these are supplemented from winter's store of root vegetables, apples, onions, and winter squashes. At the Ecole Bilingue, the school garden program follows the seasonal rhythms of a *potager*, in the hope of establishing the same connection between the earth and daily life that the *potager* does in France.

The school garden is located on a corner opposite the classroom buildings, on the grounds of Kona Kai Organic Farm, a large urban garden that has been in existence since 1994. The farm's founder, Michael Norton, lends the school three raised beds, each about four

feet wide and forty feet long. The spirit of community that is engendered by Michael Norton and his staff is an important part of the gardening experience for the children. They see themselves as part of a larger unit, as they observe people at work in the garden beds around them. Occasionally, the children are asked if they would like to help harvest carrots for the farm, or to help weed one of the farm's beds, thereby becoming participants in the workings of the farm itself. Whenever the children are at Kona Kai, they see people coming to buy the farm's organic produce, which is not unlike what they themselves are growing. The middle school at Ecole Bilingue has three raised beds near its classrooms. These are planted first in fall, and the process from sowing to harvest, including a unit on recycling and composting, is incorporated into the science curriculum for grades six through eight. In addition, there are two large planter boxes on the school's premises just outside the kindergarten classrooms, each two feet wide and four feet long. Finally, a raised bed containing a fragrant herb garden planted with rosemary, lavender, mint, thyme, and sage stands in the school's central courtyard, where it is a focal point. The children have been taught to brush against the herbs to release their scent, and to compare the resinous potency of rosemary, for example, with the delicate onion aroma of chive blossoms.

Aroma

Aroma, odor, scent. These are the olfactory sensations or impressions we have when we eat or drink something. For example, when you eat an orange, its perfume fills your mouth. If you swallow without taking time to savor it (see Taste, page 4), the scent has no time to be released. The orange will have no taste.

These precious aromas, which are largely responsible for the unique personalities of different fruits and vegetables, are fragile. They are comprised of very volatile ingredients. The first piece of advice to give any future epicurean—on condition that you put it into practice yourself—is to take the time to chew what you eat as well as to take the time to truly taste what you drink.

Also very important: the aromas, hence the flavorings, released by a food or drink change depending on whether the food or drink is cold or hot. One typical example: some people who like chicken when it's served hot do not care for chicken when served cold. The aromas and flavors are different.

—From *Le Goût et L'Enfant (Taste and the Child)*
by Jacques Puisais

Since the school garden site is permanent, and the only changes that occur with the new school year are the children's grade levels, the plots remain the same, with each class having an assigned area. Gardening lessons have been increased from one every other week to once a week. The first lessons of the fall term focus on familiarizing the students with their new garden, sampling the season's fruits and vegetables and then preparing for winter and spring. An organized tomato tasting is held, during which the children sample seven or eight different varieties, some of which they have grown themselves.

The students are asked to notice the texture, juice content, and density of the flesh; the color; the smell; and the taste of each of the tomatoes, and then to describe what they observe. They are encouraged to think of all the ways tomatoes can be eaten—salads, sauces, stuffed, grilled—and to think of specific dishes in which tomatoes are used, such as pizza, pasta, and salsa.

When the children return to school after vacation, they view their garden, now overflowing with late-summer bounty, in wonder and astonishment. The plots have a whimsical look, with ten-foot-tall sunflower stalks, secret patches of strawberries, beans vining up poles, random onions and garlic pushing up through the soil, and smatterings of orange marigolds and pink and white cosmos. The children are responsible not only for harvesting tomatoes, beans, eggplants, basil, and cilantro, but also for tidying the garden by removing weeds and plants that are dead or no longer bearing vegetables or fruits. These faded plants were deliberately left in the garden over the summer, so that when the students returned they would have the opportunity to observe the full life cycle. Arugula and lettuce plants, sown in spring and whose tender leaves were used in salads, have metamorphosed. The once delicately flavored arugula leaves are now bitter and tough, and the usually compact plant is tall and branching. Lettuce plants have become towering cones as tall as some of the children, each one topped with a fluffy seed head.

Since the school garden is a year-round *potager*, planting for a fall and winter harvest occurs at the same time the vegetables and herbs of summer are being harvested. One of the earliest activities in the garden after returning to school is the planting of winter greens—chard, lettuces, spinach—and winter roots such as beets, carrots, radishes, and turnips. Garlic and onion bulbs are covered with soil, as are crocus and daffodil bulbs for future bouquets. Planting ahead is important, because as the season changes, so will the garden's content. Maintaining the children's interest in the garden is important, too, and one way to do that is to have a garden that produces continuously.

During the weekly gardening lessons, students are often side-tracked by the abundance of small creatures, whether aphids, earth-worms, or caterpillars. They are taught that these inhabitants can be either beneficial or destructive, and are shown how to safely rid their garden of the destructive visitors and encourage the beneficial ones.

The garden is a place to have fun, where the soil holds secrets, the plants are producers, and the thrill of harvesting overrides a dislike for spinach or radishes. Children who were once vocal in their dislike of vegetables will clamor to harvest just as many beans and lettuce leaves as their classmates. When gardening lessons have ended for the day, the students, often covered with dirt but full of pride in their accomplishments, return to their classes, ready to plan their next harvest or the meal they hope to make.

Originally the garden project was managed by classroom teachers and parent volunteers, but now there is a garden director, a part-time staff member who is responsible for the care and upkeep of the garden, the gardening and cooking lessons, and coordinating garden-related classroom activities with the curriculum being presented by other teachers. Students in kindergarten through third grade meet every week in the garden with the garden director. During the summer, volunteer parents maintain and harvest the garden.

Future plans include expanding access to preschool classes through fifth grade, and creating a garden on the school's own growing premises, which would be landscaped with fruit trees. The dream is to one day have a garden in which the children tend and harvest the vegetables and fruits that are prepared in the school's kitchen for lunch.

The French Way with Food

Denise Moullé, an expert on French food and culture, offers her perspective on the relationship the French have with their food and their land.

France is the largest agricultural exporter in Europe, and small farmers are still an important part of that statistic. Their presence is due in large measure to the government's support of small and average-sized farms. In contrast to the United States, farmers with forty to sixty acres enjoy a decent income from their land, and the central government offers subsidies to encourage them to grow high-quality foods that bring good returns at the market.

The French are still very closely tied to their land. Even city dwellers feel this connection. Most people have a cousin, an uncle, or a grandparent living in the country, whom they visit regularly. They go to prepare preserves for the winter, to bottle wine made from grapes picked on the spot, to can vegetables, and to make sausages, pâtés, and confits. Children have fond memories of these days, or even whole summers, spent in the country at their relatives' farms.

Many French people have their own gardens. It is always a pleasure to see the small, well-tended plots at the front or the back of homes, many of them planted with both flowers and vegetables. Neighbors can often be seen standing amid the rows, comparing notes on what they have sown. When arriving by train in a large city, it is wonderful to travel past the suburban gardens. Cities give free land out beyond their boundaries, and a lot of workers who can't afford a house with a garden maintain a parcel in these outskirts, bicycling to it every day to tend their vegetables. These gardens are always carefully cared for, with the tidy rows of vegetables and flowers and the absence of weeds giving testament to the pride each gardener feels.

The importance of gardens to the French is matched by the central role daily meals play in their lives. In spite of the increase in fast-food restaurants and huge supermarkets in French cities, many people continue to take most of their meals at home. Lunch is still the main meal of the day, and many working people and children make a point of returning home for it. Even meals taken at work or at school in cafeteria-style restaurants are carefully balanced, and are often an opportunity to have a chat with a friend. It is always fun to read the menus of the lunches offered in French schools, for they sound like those one sees in expensive restaurants—shredded carrot salad, *steak frites*, cheese, and fruit. It is hard for French people to get together without sharing a repast. Relationships with family or friends are naturally built around meals. Indeed, it is common to invite people over to share a meal at home, and usually close friends or family members drop in around lunch or dinner because they are sure to find someone home and they know that the food will be graciously shared.

Meals are a ceremony. There is a prescribed order in which the food is served, and even a simple meal is never rushed, as it is the prime time to share the day. Although a very large number of women work in France, they have maintained the tradition of going home after work and cooking dinner, although the meals are not as elaborate as they were twenty years ago. Special meal preparations are reserved for weekends, when most people gather for a large, long meal. But the daily meals are still very much part of family life.

Food is so important to the French way of life that it is not uncommon for people to plan a weekend around visiting a certain area for its gastronomic offerings. They research restaurants, pinpoint farms for their special products, and check to see where a province's culinary traditions can best be explored. Of course, it is now possible to eat a dish from Provence in Alsace and vice versa, but it will not be as good as when you eat it locally. The ingredients will be different, the spices will not be just right.

French children grow up hearing a lot about food. It is a common subject of conversation at the table, where men and women alike gather to compare recipes and sources, and to exchange information on new culinary discoveries.

The local markets are very animated and interesting. In large cities, open markets can be found every day of the week, while in the villages, there are weekly open markets. At all of these, the French are very discriminating about their providers. They usually buy from the same people, selecting a favorite butcher, baker, and vegetable vendor. They build relationships with these market sellers, and they exchange family news, as well as pick up solid advice on what to buy that is special to that day or season. Thus, the markets serve two purposes, as places to buy good-quality food and to socialize with the sellers and other buyers. Many small-town employers allow their employees to take time off to go to the market the day it is in town, a practice that helps to maintain this important French tradition.

Although large cities are struggling to keep some old customs alive, smaller French towns are meeting this challenge with greater success. Residents are fearful of too much modernization threatening traditional ways of life, so they are actively encouraging the growth of organic farming. Indeed, today there is a heartening emphasis on a return to natural agriculture and the rediscovery of long-forgotten heirloom vegetables and fruits.

CHAPTER TWO

In the Children's Garden

$\mathcal{E}$NTHUSIASM AND REGULAR PARTICIPATION from both parents or teachers and children are needed for the success of a small kitchen garden at home or school, whether in the ground, in raised beds, or in containers. In this chapter we offer some suggestions for ways to initiate, maintain, and harvest a children's kitchen garden with simple activities that enable adults, even those without prior gardening experience, to become guides and partners in the world of gardening and taste.

The garden of the Ecole Bilingue and the activities that occur there can act as a model for starting a garden at home or at your child's school. Home gardens, however, offer much more time and opportunity for discovering and exploring the relationship between the earth and the food we eat than a school garden can. In the kitchen at home, preparing food, tasting it, and, above all, sharing meals, are daily experiences, not class lessons. At home, it is the parent who daily guides the child in the gardening process and in developing an evaluative sense of taste, and it can be an enriching experience for both.

While a kitchen garden can be started almost any time of year, spring is often the best choice. The dormant winter season is drawing to a close and the colors of the outdoors are beginning to change from brown and gray to bright green. When the first shoots of spring grasses push up from the soil and the trees begin to show their earliest leaves, children and adults are naturally seized by the desire to plant a garden.

Soil

A healthy garden soil can be viewed as a living entity. At any time, an uncountable number of animals, ranging in size from beetles and earthworms down to microbes, are going through their life cycles, generation following generation. The plant kingdom is represented not just by the plants readily visible, but also by small weeds, by millions of tiny seeds, most of them invisible, and by the ever-present fungi that are decomposing the plant particles.

At the same time, there are innumerable chemical reactions occurring in the soil atmosphere, next to the roots, and along the surface of the soil particles. Old plant parts, under constant microbial attack, are decomposing into their primary elements. Molecules are continuously moving back and forth between the soil solids and the soil solution, while the roots are ceaselessly removing water and nutrients and giving off carbon dioxide.

The initial decisions surrounding the establishment of the garden are based on practical considerations. The site needs a minimum of six hours of full sun, although a full day of sun is most desirable, ready access to water, and suitable soil. The location can be chosen jointly with the children, especially those six years old and older, with the adult explaining why one site is more appropriate than another, and what kind of environment is necessary for vegetables to grow and thrive. The size of the garden is determined by the available space, and by the time and effort everyone wishes to commit to the project.

Once the site has been selected, the work of readying the ground for planting offers a myriad of opportunities for children to become physically involved in the development of the garden. Weed pulling and hoeing are delightedly done by children, especially when they understand that removing weeds, turning the soil, and preparing a seed bed are preludes to the success of their garden. They will gladly cover themselves in dirt as they pull up small weeds or chop them down with a child-sized hoe, or plunge their hands into the freshly dug ground, only to discover an earthworm burrowing through the soil. The sense of accomplishment at having created a weed-free patch of earth and then imagining it full of luscious vegetables is shared by children and adults alike.

This early participation in the garden, even if adults are doing the real work, can show children how labor is needed to make the plot flourish. From the very beginning, they develop a sense of the importance of the nurturing and caretaking of living things. Children are quick to notice a stray weed, a big clump of soil, or a pesky invader. To reinforce this notion, child-sized tools, which can be handled and manipulated without adult assistance, are useful and the source of great pride. A small watering can and hand trowel; child-sized hoes, shovels, and rakes; and a special hose nozzle with an easy-to-manage sprinkler head all are good choices, although many a seed has been planted using only a strong spoon.

If the choice is a container garden, include the children in the trip to the nursery to purchase potting mix and containers, engaging them in the decision on what to buy. Readying the potting mix for planting is a wonderful job for a child, as dry matter is transformed into a lush dark planting medium with only the addition of water, a delightfully messy job that welcomes little hands.

Finally, when the garden has been readied, it is time to plant. Planting a seed is an act of faith. It is difficult for a child (and often for an adult as well) to believe that the small dry thing in his or her hand has within it the germ of life to grow and become a plant whose leaves and roots and fruits will provide food. It is exciting to see the first leaves, even of a humble radish, emerge from the soil. No matter how many times it is repeated, nor how old the gardener is, a sense of satisfaction and pleasure comes from protecting the first leaves from marauders while the root grows, and finally grasping the top and pulling forth from the soil a beautiful red-and-white radish. The knowledge that a tiny seed turns into a hearty plant, and finally into something edible, is the foundation of an education about food, taste, and cooking that a child will draw upon throughout his or her lifetime.

The adult guides in the selection of what seeds, bulbs, tubers, and seedlings to plant in the garden during which season, taking into consideration what would be interesting to have for the kitchen harvest. Larger seeds have characteristics that make them especially good for small children to plant. They are easy to handle with tiny hands in the process of developing dexterity, and nearly all are quick to germinate. Because of their size, they are planted deeper than smaller seeds, where they thrive on more moisture and bring early success to the garden. In spring, late summer, and early fall, the cool seasons, large-seeded radishes, peas, beets, spinach, and chard, along with nasturtiums, are good choices for sowing, while early summer is the time to plant large-seeded squashes, summer beans, sunflowers, corn, and pumpkin.

Some smaller seeds, such as those for lettuces and carrots, can be quick to germinate, but others like eggplant may take much longer. Because of their small size—lettuce has over a thousand seeds per ounce—such seeds are difficult to plant singly, so scatter plant-

ing is an alternative. For scatter planting, seeds can be held in the hand or on a dish or saucer, and then, using a thumb and index finger, lightly sprinkled or scattered across the surface of the soil, rather than planted singly in a row. They are then covered with soil, generally to a depth of a quarter inch. As the plants grow, they are thinned to the desired distance. In many instances, the thinnings can be incorporated into salads or soups or used as seasonings. Children enjoy the sense of abandon that scatter planting initially engenders, and later, when the seedlings have emerged, like to be meticulous when thinning. But this method of shallow planting makes it more difficult to maintain the moisture in the soil on the warm days that are necessary for germination. A task for a child might be to sprinkle the seedbed daily, using a watering can. An adult should be ultimately responsible, however, as both inadequate water and too much water can cause the seeds to fail to germinate. In spring and fall, small-seeded lettuces and carrots are good choices for planting, while in early summer, cilantro, dill, and basil can be put into the soil along with tomatoes, and a little later, when the soil has warmed, eggplants and peppers.

Children enjoy planting onions, garlic, potatoes, and flower bulbs. They are large and easy to handle, and much deeper holes are needed than those for seeds. Also, cutting potatoes into eyes to plant or putting tiny onions or cloves of garlic into holes is appealing because what a child sticks into the earth is so clearly related to what will come forth from it. Since these plantings have inside them the nutrients for a very strong start, they are usually very successful. Potatoes can be planted in spring through early summer, while onions and garlic are planted in spring or, in mild winter climates, in fall. Crocus and daffodil bulbs are planted in fall and dahlia bulbs in early summer.

Seedlings of numerous vegetables, herbs, and flowers can be purchased in season from garden centers and nurseries, usually with colored markers depicting the mature plant. This makes for easy shopping with children because they can choose what they would like to see in their garden. Transplants are an excellent choice for those vegetables that are difficult or time-consuming to germinate in the garden, or for planting in areas with short growing seasons. Select small, well-formed seedlings with healthy green leaves. Larger seedlings may be root-bound from having been too long in the tray or container, and thus may never develop the healthy roots needed by a mature plant. Planting seedlings is a garden activity children of all ages can accomplish: digging holes, pulling plants from trays and soaking them, slipping the root balls into the holes, and gently packing the soil around them.

After a few basic decisions, it is time to shop and to plant. It is exciting to look at the pictures of luscious vegetables or beautiful flowers on seed packets or in catalogs and then try to imagine them in your own garden. The trick is not what to plant, but how much to dare to plant. Everything looks so full of promise. Within the limits of seasonality, the children can make their own choices, which will reinforce their sense of responsibility and open the way for tasting and enjoying their vegetables. When a squash begins with a picture on a seed packet, is planted, nourished, blooms, and bears fruit, all under the caring hand of a child, it is nigh impossible for the child not to want to taste and exclaim over the product of his or her labor.

Once the planting occurs, the seed packets, bulb pictures, and seedling markers can be incorporated into a garden notebook that can be used to make weather, garden, and tasting notes and to record favorite recipes from the garden's bounty. Such comments can be simple, yet telling, providing a record of the garden experience not unlike classic gardeners' yearbooks. "Good tomatoes. We'll buy these next year, too." "Rain washed away all my lettuce seed, so didn't get to taste any." "These radishes were really good when they were little, but they got too hot later." "Tomato Sauce: Cook chopped tomatoes in a little olive oil with some garlic and herbs until they are soft and saucy. Pour over spaghetti noodles or any kind of noodles or ravioli."

Manure

Manure may be purchased in composted form from nurseries and garden centers, with steer manure the most commonly available type. Composted manure can be dug directly into the garden at the time of planting or any time thereafter, and we recommend it for use in children's gardens.

Hot manure, which is raw and has not been fully composted, can be purchased directly from stables or farms, but it must be dug into the garden at least a month before the garden site is planted. It should be handled only by adults, and with care. For safety reasons, we do not recommend its use in children's gardens.

Green Gulch

At Green Gulch Organic Farm, the children have a first-hand farm-to-market experience. First, the tour guide gives each child a half-pint berry basket lined with a paper towel. The children head over to the currant bushes, where they are shown how to pick the ripest berries for the farmers to sell at the market the following day. The currant bushes are nearly as tall as the seven and eight year olds, who scramble to find the reddest fruits. Small hands reach deep into the bushes, and more than one berry is popped into a child's mouth before it can reach a basket. Once the baskets are filled and set aside, the children head over to a bamboo grove. Here they are encouraged to pull strips of bamboo from the towering stalks and are taught how to make rice packages that can be filled with cooked rice.

Involving children early in the process and keeping them involved as growth progresses toward harvest is a key to their ongoing interest in the garden. In home gardens, daily attendance involves inspection to see if the first shoots have yet appeared, and to observe any changes from one day to the next. This can be reinforced by making a chart to see how much certain plants grow. A child can measure them every few days and mark down the date and their size.

Adequate moisture is needed to make plants grow, and watering engages all of a child's senses. The sight of the water first coming from a sprinkler, the little sound it makes as it hits the ground, the smell of it on damp earth, the feel of it on bare arms and legs, the taste of it when drunk from the hose, and, of course, the possibility of mud, all combine to make watering a favored garden job for most children. It is also something that a child can do independently, or nearly so, and it is a powerful aspect of the nurturing of plants.

Another aspect of plant nurturing is the use of compost or fertilizer. A well-fertilized plant has lustrous dark green leaves; one that is not will have dull, lighter green leaves and may show yellowing. These are visual clues that children can look for on their own or with an adult on their regular inspections of the garden. At the same time, they can try to spot any signs of insect problems or damage, as one of the most effective ways to control insects in the garden is to react before they do extensive harm, which can happen in two or three days, or even overnight.

Fertilizing to provide nutrients is an opportunity for parents to teach children about natural gardening. Decomposed manure and organic compost are sources of some of the nutrients needed by plants, and they are natural products of our environment. The recycling of manure and organic matter back into the soil teaches children about replenishing the earth that in turn feeds and nourishes their growing bodies. If a compost pile is not possible at home or at school, compost is easily purchased at nurseries or garden centers, as is decomposed manure. Manure is always an enticing subject for children, and they consider it quite daring and adventuresome to put composted chicken or steer manure in the garden. There are lessons to be learned from manure about composition and decomposition, about how elements pass back and forth between the plant and animal kingdom. Similar lessons come from using a compost pile as a source of fertilizer (see page 25). Having a special container in the kitchen for potato peels, coffee grounds, eggshells—in short anything that is organic—and then giving a child the job of dumping it on the compost pile is one way to illustrate the concept vividly. Reactions might initially be "Yuk! I'm not touching that gross stuff!" But with assistance and explanation, the disgust will give way to interest and enthusiasm. A revelation will occur when the garbage from the kitchen has miraculously decomposed and become dark, rich earth to return to the garden.

Insects are a source of fascination for children and, like the manure and compost, demonstrate the connection between the plant and animal kingdoms. Their presence in the garden can be spotted by the appearance of bud or leaf damage or discoloration. Finding the culprits is like detective work, and given a small magnifying glass, children can busily peer under leaves and press their faces near the earth in search of any invaders. A close inspection will more often than not reveal tiny insects such as aphids and whiteflies feeding on the succulent undersides of the leaves. Big bites out of the greenery might well signal larger insects like beetles, caterpillars, or snails. Chances are the offenders are still on the plant and can be captured by the little gardener, accompanied by shouts of "Look what I found, look what I found in the garden! What is it?" The questions may come in the form of a bombardment, but like so much else in the garden, they are an opportunity to discover more. Examining the insect and making a drawing of it, being careful to note the coloration, and counting the legs and antennae and other details, is a prelude to looking it up in a common garden pest book and discovering its name, feeding habits, and life cycle.

Many insect problems can be treated with fresh water, as a spray of water with the hose will wash them off. Aphids can be discouraged by spraying a dilute mixture of liquid dish soap on the affected

Next, the children are shown the compost piles in all their stages. Familiar with composting because of their experience at Kona Kai, the children are curious about what is in the Green Gulch pile. They see coffee grounds and eggshells and remnants of meals, in contrast to the Kona Kai compost, which is primarily made of discarded vegetables and greenery. The braver children stick their hands into the piles, getting close enough to feel the heat of the decomposing vegetation. They know what is happening and proudly share their knowledge of composting with the guide.

The tour then continues through the expansive herb garden, the cold frames where seedlings are started, and finally to the beds of greens and other vegetables.

areas, a job children enjoy. Two tablespoons of soap to a quart of water is adequate. Some problems like caterpillars and snails can be resolved by hand-picking the creatures from the plants and relocating them elsewhere. Sending pests to the far corner of the yard, or down the street to an empty lot, is undertaken with passion by children as they guard their garden against hungry marauders.

Not everything planted succeeds, so a key element to a successful garden is learning why something failed and solving the problem. This is especially important when children are involved. Few things are more discouraging than inspecting the garden every day and seeing nothing come up. Rather than giving up, though, the next step is to find out why. If bean seeds haven't put forth sprouts after a week, it is time to investigate. With a child observing, carefully dig down into the soil with a knife to see if indeed the bean seed you planted is still there. Did it start to sprout and then die? Is there evidence of insect damage? Did the seed rot? All of these are possible reasons for the lack of a sprout, and the process of investigating is an effective approach to teaching children about problem solving. The next step is to replant, this time with the knowledge that too much water caused the seed to rot, or that not enough water caused the emerging seedling to die, or that ravenous insects need to be controlled. If snails are eating young shoots, a child can be taught how to make a barrier of vermiculite or gravel to protect the seedlings. Gardening is about problem solving, not failure. Everyone can have a green thumb.

When gardening with children, especially young ones, it is important to provide them with a sense of purpose, and in a vegetable garden this means tasting as soon as possible. Eating the harvest is the point of a vegetable garden. Some vegetables can be harvested throughout their growth cycle, not only at a single moment of ripeness. Peas are such a vegetable.

Peas offer an especially enticing gardening and taste experience. They are not only edible at all stages of growth, but at each stage they have different tastes and textures to explore, and each requires a slightly different treatment in the kitchen. Pea shoots, once they

are three or four inches tall, can be clipped and eaten raw in a salad. Their taste is tender and sweetly vegetative. The white blossoms are edible, too, rapidly followed by the developing pea pods. Crunchy and crisp, the very young pods are intensely sweet and can be eaten whole. Children love to pick these off the vine and munch on them right in the garden as they admire the plants or look for insects. At the next stage, the peas inside the pod begin to swell. In some varieties, both the peas and their pods can be eaten (called *mangetouts*, meaning "eat all" in French), while in others, the pod rapidly becomes too tough and stringy to enjoy, and the peas instead are shelled.

These very young and tender peas can be eaten raw or treated to only a brief cooking. As the peas mature further, their sugar begins to convert to starch and they become mealy. At this point they are ideal for turning into a thick and creamy soup. Mature pods that are left on the vine will dry, where they can be collected and fully dried for cooking much later, or saved for seed to replant the following year.

In French kitchen gardens, spinach is given pride of place and considered a delicacy, unlike in the United States, where it has a negative connotation, especially among children. Part of its appeal in the French home is due to the way in which it is cooked and seasoned. First leaves are well washed, then briefly steamed or parboiled before being drained and cooked with butter, shallots, salt, and pepper, plus a little nutmeg. Puréed, with a little cream added, this dish is one of the earliest solid foods fed to French infants, and is a favorite among French adults as well.

As part of the garden-to-table process, spinach can be harvested and brought into the kitchen by the young gardener. Encouraging children to smell the nutmeg and think about what other foods might be seasoned with it, to taste the butter for the spinach, and to watch the leaves cook to the perfect bright green involves the child in the creative process of cooking and in the notion of what makes food taste the way it does. The child can stir in the butter and the seasoning, and push the button on the blender, watching the spinach whirl into a creamy purée. Tasting a spoonful of the final dish, and then deciding if a touch more salt or pepper might be needed, is an evaluative process that is only developed through experience. At last, the dish is ready, and in the process it has become a personal creation of the child. Fresh, flavorful, newly harvested garden spinach, deftly cooked into a well-seasoned light purée, served on a colorful platter, and garnished with a bit of hard-boiled egg or toasted croutons, is a portrait of the child's pride in the kitchen garden, from the planting of the seeds to the harvest, and finally to the cooking.

COMPOST

COMPOST, WHICH IS decomposed organic material, is used in the garden to improve the soil, provide vital elements to the plants, and to recycle nutrients that would otherwise be wasted. It improves the soil primarily by adding organic matter, which increases soil porosity so that air and water can travel easily and roots can grow readily. The organic matter continues to break down for a year or more, constantly making more minerals available for plant growth.

Aerobic composting, in which organic material is decomposed by microbes into new organic compounds, can be done easily by children, with beneficial effects for the garden and their education.

The compost pile is started with plant material, perhaps weeds and cuttings cleared from the garden site or kitchen scraps. The plants or scraps should be chopped or broken into pieces of less than an inch, because small pieces decompose more rapidly. The microbes in the pile need water and oxygen, so the pile should be kept moist but not soggy, and it must be aerated. If the pile is loose enough, the oxygen can pass through it, but it may need to be turned regularly to ensure good aeration.

A moist, loose compost pile should heat up within a few days and stay hot for sev-

eral weeks. The interior temperature will be well over 100° and should be quite evident. It can be checked with your hand, a thermometer, or with a metal bar left thrust into the center of the pile. The pile should be monitored at least once a week, and more often if possible, so that when the temperature begins to fall it can be corrected. Falling interior temperatures indicate a decrease in microbial activity. At first this drop is caused by insufficient moisture or oxygen, so the pile should be opened and examined. Water should be added if needed and the pile turned to aerate it.

After several weeks the pile will have reduced in size and the decomposition will be very evident. At this point, the temperature will drop, and turning and watering the pile will have almost no effect because almost all the plant material has decomposed. The pile should be cured for another few weeks, that is, properly aerated and then left to sit. After that, it can be worked into soil before planting.

CHAPTER THREE

Digging In

THIS CHAPTER WILL ENABLE even a novice gardener to embark with confidence on building an education about food, taste, cooking, and the quality of ingredients via the garden. It opens with information that supplements what was presented in the preceding chapter on establishing and maintaining a garden, and includes a short discussion on seasonality.

Then, profiles of different plants—vegetables, flowers, and strawberries—follow, each annotated with information on planting season, planting directions, germination time, general care, a description of what to expect as the plant grows and matures, harvesting methods, and a few simple kitchen ideas. Although general days to maturity and harvest are given as guidelines, some vegetables differ dramatically from one variety to another in this area, so in reading seed catalogs or choosing seed packets or transplants at a nursery, check the individual varieties for their days to harvest. For more specific information about the area in which you live, ask your local nursery staff to suggest suitable varieties.

The description of what to expect as a plant grows is especially helpful because it enables the parent or teacher to recognize the changing signs of a plant's growth cycle and thus be able to show and discuss them with a child. These insights help both adults and children learn to spot the prime moment for harvest, knowing that the glossy skin of an eggplant, for example, indicates it is at its peak of flavor, while a dull and wrinkled surface means it is past its prime. When these garden lessons are brought into the kitchen, samples of underripe, ripe, and overripe vegetables can be observed, tasted, and compared, so that children learn that the quality of food is directly related to how it is grown and when it is harvested.

With the exception of strawberries, the following plants are all annuals, completing their life cycle within a year, and most can be grown in containers. Some are started from seeds sown directly in the garden, while others are a product of transplanted seedlings. All are easy to grow, and the selections are meant to give you ideas and inspirations about what you might want to grow and cook with your children. Although the list of fruits and vegetables does not include every possibility, each season is well represented, giving the gardener planting and harvesting options throughout the year. Virtually anything fresh from the garden, harvested at its peak of flavor, is going to be satisfying. Even eating a freshly pulled carrot or green onion, the aroma of the earth still about it, is the stuff of memories. Potatoes for oven fries and thick soups, tomatoes and basil for salads and sauces, corn and beans to slather with an herb butter, strawberries for jams and crêpes, and plump summer squash to stuff and bake are all options, but there are many more, as you and your children will discover.

Taste is a friend of freedom. Forbidding certain foods (when they are not dangerous) is as inefficient as forcing children to eat others.

—From *Le Goût et L'Enfant (Taste and the Child)*
by Jacques Puisais

A garden isn't defined by precise parameters. It may consist of a single tomato plant growing in a pot, a collection of lettuces sown in a small patch in a backyard, or a dozen different vegetables each represented by a dozen plants laid out in a large space. There are no hard-and-fast rules. A garden represents a personal choice informed by space, time, and the energy one wants to commit to tending it.

One can enjoy the excitement of a single tomato plant growing and putting out more and more leaves, then the appearance of the first blossoms with their promise of fruits to come. A child's nurturing regime of watering and fertilizing is as important for a single plant as it is for a hundred. One homegrown tomato plant can provide dozens of tomatoes for tastings; ingredients for salads, sauces, soups, stews, and sandwiches; and many opportunities for teaching and learning with children. What is important in the garden is not its size, but experiencing and sharing the connection between the earth and what we eat.

Choosing and Preparing a Garden Site

Several basic requirements define a good garden site. It must receive adequate light, as few vegetables or herbs will thrive with less than 6 hours a day of direct sun. The ground must be fertile enough to support the growth of the plants, and there must be ready access to water.

Look over the area in which you envision your garden. Is something already growing there? That's a good sign, because it indicates the ground is fertile enough to support some kind of plant life. Look at the color of the soil. Black or dark brown is often an indicator of fertile soil. If it is red or yellow, you will likely need to add amendments. Bags of organic compost or steer manure purchased from garden centers or nurseries will help, and can be added once you begin working the soil.

Let water run on the site. Does it "sheet," collecting in puddles and pools, or is it absorbed? Pooling indicates that your soil may need to be loosened to improve drainage. If your site is on a slope or a slight incline, observe the flow of the water and design your garden to run across rather than down the slope, so that the water will be absorbed.

Is the site windy? If so, you may need to provide protection from the wind, as it is drying and damaging, especially to young plants and seedlings.

Once you have chosen a site, dealing with weeds is the next step. First, any visible weeds must be removed, then the weed seeds in the soil must be germinated and their seedlings pulled. It is much easier to work moist soil, so water the area thoroughly, preferably with a sprinkler, two or three days before you begin weeding. If the site has large weeds with big stems, chop them down with a hoe. Dig out any large roots with a shovel.

Turn over the soil with a shovel to a depth of about one foot. Remove large roots and any large rocks or chunks of cement, concrete, or other unwanted matter.

Once the garden site has been prepared and the ground is bare, water again to germinate weed seeds in the soil. When the weed seedlings are about an inch high, remove them with a hoe or turn them under. Use a garden fork to break up clods and chunks and to work in compost or decomposed manure. Rake the site smooth.

Now lay out the garden. You can divide it into squares, rectangles, rows straight or wavy, or any variation you desire. Leave footpaths along the sides and/or through the middle, so that every part of the garden can be easily reached. The planting areas, whatever their configuration, can be mounded for easy drainage into beds six to eight inches high, with watering ditches or furrows between rows or around squares, rectangles, or circles.

Sowing Seeds and Transplanting Seedlings

To plant seeds, follow the directions concerning depth, spacing, and maintenance that accompany each plant profile in this chapter.

If you are using seedlings, soak them, still in their pots or trays, in a bucket of water until their potting mix is saturated. Make a hole in the ground, then gently remove the seedling from its container, keeping the roots and their potting soil mix intact. Put the seedling in the prepared hole, and fill the hole with the loose soil removed from it, tamping it in firmly around the roots. Gently water the planted seedlings to settle the soil around the roots and to provide moisture to encourage growth. Use this same procedure if transplanting seedlings into containers.

Watering and Fertilizing

When seeds are first planted, keep the soil immediately around them moist until they have germinated. Shallow-planted seeds may need to be watered more than those planted more deeply because the soil layer closer to the surface loses water to evaporation more rapidly than deeper soil layers. Once the seeds have germinated, they need water in the area around their roots. Test the soil moisture by digging down into the root zone. If the soil surface is dry but the root zone is still quite moist, the plant does not need water. Add water only as the root zone dries. Overwatering can kill plants because it deprives them of the oxygen they need. How often you water depends upon the soil, what you have planted, the climate, and weather conditions.

Heavy clay soils hold more water than lighter or sandier soils, and require less watering. As the plants grow and add more leaf surface, they will require more water. Wind and hot weather will speed the loss of soil moisture, which will need to be replaced.

Fertilize your plants as needed. If you have fertilized your garden well with compost or manure, you should not need to add more until you plant your second crop. At that time, dig in more compost or manure.

Controlling Pests

Garden pests such as insects, snails, birds, and caterpillars are a curiosity for children, but they also cause problems for growing plants. The first step in controlling pests is to keep the garden free of weeds and the plants healthy. A second line of defense is to hand-pick and remove pests the moment they are spotted. This can be effective for larger culprits such as snails, caterpillars, and tomato worms. It is not feasible for small interlopers, however, such as aphids, whiteflies, and cabbage loopers. Spraying plants with water helps to dislodge aphids and they can be controlled with a dilute mixture of liquid dish soap (see page 21). Sticky insect traps work on aphids and whiteflies as does the introduction of beneficial insects such as lady-

How Does a Seed Start to Grow?

To show children the first stages of a seed becoming a plant, line a clear plastic cup with black construction paper that has been thoroughly soaked in water. Although other colors of paper may be used, the emerging seedlings show up clearly against the black background. Slip a selection of about half a dozen different seeds between the plastic and the paper, spacing them about $1/2$ inch apart. Keep the paper moist, and after about a week, the seeds will begin to sprout. This is a lesson the Ecole Bilingue uses to introduce kindergartners to the gardening program.

Egg-Carton Seedlings

Children can start their own seedlings in egg-carton trays for transplanting into a garden. Fill each egg cup with moist potting mix. Following the planting instructions in Chapter 3, place the seeds at the correct depth and cover loosely with more moist potting mix. Set the seed trays in a sunny place, and keep the seeds moist until they germinate. Once the plants have reached a height of 2 to 4 inches and have at least six leaves, transplant them into a garden or a container.

bugs. The garden has many beneficial residents in addition to ladybugs. Watch for praying mantises, ladybugs, and, of course, earthworms, which enrich and aerate the soil as they pass through it.

Planting in Containers

Planting vegetables and herbs in containers is a viable alternative to preparing garden ground, as long as other conditions—adequate light, water, and fertilizer—are met. Start by selecting a container large enough to allow for the anticipated root growth of the vegetable you choose. The container must also have a hole in the bottom to allow drainage.

Put together a potting mixture using approximately two-thirds organic potting mix and one-third sand, and thoroughly soak it with water. Fill the container with the mix to within a half inch of the rim. Then, follow the directions for planting seeds included with each plant in this chapter, or, if you are planting seedlings, follow the directions on page 30.

Since the potting mix has no nutrients, they will need to be added. Apply a dilute solution of balanced naturally derived liquid fertilizer, such as fish emulsion, to seedlings after the first two leaves, known as the cotyledon leaves, have appeared, and to transplanted seedlings at the time of planting. Repeat every week or ten days thereafter for most vegetables.

Seasonality

The seasonality of vegetables refers to the stage of growth at which the plant is harvested for the table. The three stages are juvenile, reproductive, and senescence. They also can be thought of as preflowering, flowering, and postflowering, respectively. After a seed germinates, the seedling emerges and begins vegetative growth, issuing an array of leaves, stems, and branches. This leafy display characterizes the juvenile stage. Lettuces, endive, cabbage, kale, arugula, and mizuna, as well as leafy-topped root vegetables such as radishes, turnips, and fennel, are all harvested at this stage.

Near the end of this rapid vegetative growth, the plant enters its reproductive period by putting up flower stalks and blooms. Artichoke buds, brussels sprouts, broccoli, and cauliflower are harvested at this stage, when they are flower buds.

After the flowers bloom and are pollinated, the plant begins to develop seed for the coming generation, and the plant ovary, which envelops the seed, ripens into a fruit. Vegetables eaten at this stage include snap beans, peas, eggplants, tomatoes, cucumbers, squashes, and peppers. Most plants bloom as the weather gets warmer. Consequently, if you want to grow a plant for its fruit as opposed to its leaves, it needs to be planted early enough in the spring to allow sufficient time to move through its various stages. For example, planting eggplants in August or September would not likely be productive, but planting lettuce would. Generally, the reverse is also true. If you want to plant a vegetable that is harvested for its vegetative growth, June or July may be too late, because the warmer temperatures speed the plant into flowering.

Beans

(Phaseolus vulgaris)

This is the common garden bean of which there are dozens and dozens of varieties, both bush and climbing types. Snap beans are meant to be eaten in the meaty green bean stage, pods and all, while others, the shelling beans, are freed from their pods when mature, and eaten either fresh or dried. Some flavorful snap bean varieties to look for are the popular old-time 'Blue Lake' and 'Kentucky Wonder,' plus 'Emerite,' a pencil-thin French bean that is very rich and meaty. All are climbers. Particularly flavorful bush beans are 'Slankette,' a thick green snap type; 'Royal Burgundy,' which has a lovely deep purple pod that turns green when cooked; and 'Roc d'Or,' a yellow-podded snap bean. Among the many types of shelling beans, the French flageolet 'Chevrier Vert' is excellent, and so is the Italian borlotto.

Season: Sow seeds or set out transplants from late spring into summer when the ground is warm, for summer and early fall harvest. Bean seeds and seedlings tend to rot in cold, wet ground.

Days to Harvest: This depends upon variety, with some early snap types ready in 45 days, and others in 55 to 65 days. Shelling beans require from 70 to 75 days on up to 90 or even 100 days, again depending upon variety.

Location: Full sun.

Containers: Bush or vining beans may be grown in containers at least 18 inches in diameter and 18 inches deep. Vining beans will require supports (see growth habit).

Germination: 5 to 7 days.

Spacing: Sow seeds 1 inch deep. Allow 4 inches between plants for bush types, and 8 inches for vining types.

Growth Habit: Bush types grow to about 2 feet and require no support. Vining types may grow to 10 feet and require support for them to twist around and climb, such as a trellis, strings along a fence, or a teepee made of sticks or other material.

What to Look For: Heart-shaped leaves appear first, followed later by white or purple blossoms (which are edible and taste like beans). Tiny beans will form after the blooms drop. Within 5 days to a week, they will be ready to pick and eat. If the beans are left on the vine, they will continue to grow and develop into mature seeds, and the plant will stop producing new blossoms and beans. Snap beans should be picked before the pods turn stringy. Shelling beans, on the contrary, should be picked when the pods have begun to wrinkle and dry slightly for fresh eating, and when the pods are quite dry if the beans are to be fully dried and stored (see sidebar).

Harvest: Hand-pick the beans.

In the Kitchen: Pencil-thin snap beans no more than 3 or 4 inches long may be eaten raw, or steam or parboil them for 3 or 4 minutes and eat them hot with a vinaigrette or a pat of herb butter (see page 87), or let them cool and add them to a salad. Larger, more mature beans will require longer cooking. A string may have developed along the pod, which can be removed by snapping back the stem and pulling downward. Simmer the beans with bacon, potatoes, and herbs, or with tomatoes, okra, and onions to make a soup.

To prepare shelling beans for cooking, remove them from their pods. Test for moisture by gently biting one. If you can bite through, cooking time may be as brief as 10 minutes. If not, they will need 20 to 30 minutes. To cook, bring them to a boil in salted water to cover, then reduce to a simmer and cook until tender. They are delicious added to soups and stews and tossed with pasta. They may also be eaten on their own or cooled and added to salads.

Drying Beans

Pick the beans when the pods and the beans are thoroughly dry, but before the pods shatter. Put the beans, pods and all, into a paper bag, then rub or thrash them, freeing the beans. The chaff will remain.

To free the beans from the chaff, toss them into the air from a straw tray. This should be done on a breezy day, so the air current will blow the chaff away, and the beans will fall back to the tray. Once the beans are free of chaff, store them in an airtight container such as a glass jar with a tightly fitting lid

Cabbage

(Brassica oleracea)

Cabbage is a stunning addition to the garden. The large outer leaves that surround the developing head are wonderfully ornamental, turning up in any color from pale green, gray, or blue green to deepest red, depending upon variety. The leaves of most cabbages are smooth to undulating, but the savoy types are covered with little puffs, like a quilt. The heads are of various shapes—round ball, flattened ball (drumhead), and conical. A reliable, flavorful conical type is 'Early Jersey Wakefield.' 'Ruby Ball' is a good choice for a red cabbage, and 'Grenadier' is a standard round green head.

Season: Sow seeds in mid- to late summer for harvest from late fall through early spring, depending upon variety. Transplants are recommended and are widely available.

Days to Harvest: This depends upon the variety, with some requiring only 60 to 65 days, and others 75 or 80 days.

Location: Full sun.

Containers: Since the plants are so large, grow only a single head in a container 18 inches deep and 12 inches in diameter.

Germination: 6 to 8 days.

Spacing: Sow seeds $1/4$ inch deep, and thin to 1 foot apart.

Growth Habit: Cupping leaves grow larger and larger to surround and protect a developing head.

What to Look For: First you will see small rounded leaves, followed by an increasing number. As the head inside begins to develop, the inner leaves will fold over one another, eventually creating a firm, solid head. As soon as the head is solid, the cabbage is ready to harvest.

Harvest: Using a sharp knife, cut the head at its base near the soil line.

In the Kitchen: Remove the large outer leaves, which are tough and strong tasting. Grate the head and mix it with mayonnaise or vinaigrette to make a salad. Add it to stir-fries, or cut it into wedges and steam them as a side dish. The wedges are especially good with corned beef and boiled potatoes served with mustard and horseradish.

Carrots

(Daucus carota)

There are many, many different carrot varieties, from walnut-sized round ones to foot-long tapered ones. An exceptionally flavorful mid-sized carrot is the French 'Touchon' variety. Longer carrots require loose, well-drained soil; if planted in clay soil, they become deformed. If your soil is heavy, choose the round or the short, blunt types to cultivate, such as the round 'Paris Market.'

Season: Sow seeds from spring through summer for harvest from late spring through summer. In areas with mild winters, sow in late summer as well, for a fall harvest. Transplants are not recommended.

Days to Harvest: This depends upon the variety, but some may be harvested when still baby size, as early as 50 days.

Location: Full sun for at least three-quarters of the day.

Containers: The round and the blunt types can be grown in containers at least 12 inches in diameter and 12 inches deep.

Germination: 6 to 8 days.

Spacing: Sow seeds a scant $1/4$ inch deep, and thin to 2 inches apart.

Growth Habit: Roots develop underground, and the leaves can grow to a foot or more tall.

What to Look For: First you will see small, feathery leaves on long stems. The stems will grow larger and larger and then thicken where they meet the growing subterranean root.

Harvest: If the soil is quite moist, small carrots can be pulled by hand. Fully mature carrots are best dug with a shovel to loosen the earth.

In the Kitchen: Carrots can be eaten raw at all stages, plain and with dips. Grate them, add a little lemon juice, olive oil, salt, and pepper, or combine grated carrots with raisins and mayonnaise to make a salad. Add $1/2$-inch pieces to stews, slice them on the diagonal in $1/4$-inch-thick pieces for stir-fries, or just steam them and add butter.

Corn

(Zea mays)

Sweet corn comes in a wealth of varieties: white, yellow, and bicolored. Some, called supersweets, have a high sugar content, while others have more starch and a more cornlike taste. Because it is pollinated by the wind, corn is best grown in blocks of four or more rows. A single row, depending upon the direction of the wind, can have the pollen blown away from it, causing small, irregular, and disappointing ears. 'Silver Queen' is a delicious white corn with a flavor well-balanced between sweet and cornlike. 'Kandy Korn' is a popular yellow, extra-sweet variety, while 'Peaches and Cream' combines kernels of both white and yellow for a sweet taste of each.

Season: Sow seeds or set out transplants in late spring and into summer when the ground is warm, for a summer harvest. Corn seeds tend to rot in cold, wet ground.

Days to Harvest: This depends upon the variety, but some early types may be harvested in 60 days, while others may take up to 110 days.

Location: Full sun.

Containers: Corn is too tall to grow easily in containers.

Germination: 5 to 7 days.

Spacing: Sow seeds 1 to 1^1/$_2$ inches deep and 6 inches apart, in rows 18 inches apart. Space transplants 6 inches apart.

Growth Habit: Corn plants have strong central stalks and long, loose flapping leaves. They grow between 5 and 7 feet tall.

What to Look For: Thin, strapping leaves appear first. Then, after considerable growth, the ears of corn emerge, initially as slender lumps in leaves along the stalk. As they enlarge, the silks extend out the ends of the leaves at the same time as the tassels develop on top of the stalk. When the tassels shed pollen, some of it will fall on the silks and, through them, pollinate the ear. The ear will continue to grow and will be ready to harvest when the silks turn brown. Occasionally the ears will develop a bulging lumpiness, with the kernels distorted and turned into large pearly gray growths by a corn fungus. Called *huitlacoche*, this fungus is considered an edible delicacy in Mexico and in upscale restaurants in the United States.

Harvest: Hand-pick, snapping the ears from the stalk.

In the Kitchen: Remove the husks and silks and boil the ears of corn, or brush them with olive oil and grill them. Or leave the ears of corn still wrapped in their husks and silks and cook over a charcoal fire. Scrape kernels of fresh corn and their milk from shucked ears and sauté them with onions, green pepper, and butter, or use them to make corn chowder.

The first day we went to the garden we took out the dead corn and put it in the compost. It's going to turn into good dirt and then we can plant more things.

—Tatiana Webb, second grade

Cucumbers

(Cucumis sativus)

The most common cucumbers are torpedo shaped with dark green skin, but round lemon cucumbers, long white varieties, and a pale green, ribbed Armenian variety are among the other slicing or salad cucumbers suitable for the garden. There are a number of pickling types as well.

Season: Sow seeds or set out transplants in late spring and into summer, when the ground is warm, for summer harvest.

Days to Harvest: This depends upon variety, but 60 to 75 days is average.

Location: Full sun.

Containers: Cucumbers may be successfully grown in containers at least 18 inches in diameter and 18 inches deep, if adequate care is given to the plants. If the cucumbers become too heavy, the vines may break. A trellis will help, but the vines will need to be well attached to it, and large cucumbers will need individual support.

Germination: 5 to 7 days.

Spacing: Sow seeds $^1/_2$ inch deep and 4 inches apart, and thin to 12 inches apart. Space transplants 12 inches apart. Three plants may be planted on mounds 24 inches in diameter.

Growth Habit: Vines can grow up to 10 feet.

What to Look For: Serrated, round, rather furry leaves sprout first, followed by small yellow blossoms, both male and female. If the blossom was fertilized, after it dries and drops, a tiny, fuzzy cucumber will develop. Within 7 to 10 days after the appearance of the fruit, the young cucumber will be ready to pick. The plant blooms from the inside out, so look for the first cucumber closest to the center of the plant; later ones form along the length of the vines as they grow.

Harvest: Use clippers or a knife to cut the fruit from the stem.

In the Kitchen: Peel and slice the cucumbers and sprinkle with salt, pepper, chopped fresh dill, and rice wine vinegar to make a salad. Combine cucumbers, tomatoes, and sweet peppers in a classic cold gazpacho. Use cucumbers in any salad, or eat them raw with a dipping sauce.

Eggplant

(Solanum melongena)

Eggplant are of two basic shapes, the globular or oval European, and the long, slender, cylindrical Asian. Although most eggplant are purple, shades of lavender exist, as do white and green, and there are particularly bitter varieties in deep red and orange that are favored for Southeast Asian stews.

Season: Sow seeds or set out transplants in late spring or early summer when the ground is warm, for harvest in mid- to late summer.

Days to Harvest: Ready after 70 to 90 days.

Location: Full sun.

Containers: Eggplants can be grown in containers at least 18 inches in diameter and 24 inches deep.

Germination: 7 to 12 days.

Spacing: Sow seeds 2 to 3 inches apart and $1/4$ inch deep, and thin to 12 inches apart. Space transplants 12 inches apart.

Growth Habit: Bushy plants grow on increasingly woody stalks to between 3 and 4 feet tall, depending upon variety and the length of the growing season.

What to Look For: The first two leaves are thin and pointed, followed by oval or roundish leaves. As the plants grow, a tinge of purple develops on the edges of the increasingly large green leaves and the stalks. The blossoms are deep lavender with a gray-green calyx, or blossom cap. When a female blossom has been pollinated, a tiny spot of color, in most cases purple, becomes apparent. As the fruit continues to grow, so does the calyx, which may have thorns.

Harvest: Eggplant may be harvested at baby size, when few seeds will have developed inside, or when mature. The skin should be shiny and glossy, not dull. Once they are dull or have begun to turn dark yellow, eggplant are past their prime. Cut from the stem with scissors or a knife.

In the Kitchen: Slice the eggplant into rounds or lengths, then brush with olive oil and sprinkle with thyme, salt, and pepper. Grill to eat hot or cold as part of a grilled vegetable platter or to use in sandwiches. Garlic mayonnaise and basil are especially good accompaniments.

Lettuce

(Latuca sativa)

Lettuce comes in many shades and shapes, from pale green to dark red, from ruffled round leaves to long, smooth ones, from loose-leaf, cylindrical heads to tightly packed spheres. There are dozens of lettuces from which to choose, each with its own distinctive appearance, taste, and texture. Many of the most colorful and flavorful lettuces are European heirlooms that have been reintroduced to the marketplace. 'Lollo Rossa' is a ruffled red loose-leaf type of Italian heritage, while 'Rouge Grenobloise' is a French Batavian that forms a large, soft head of undulating leaves of red and green. 'Merveille de Quatre Saisons' is a succulent butter head type wrapped in deep magenta leaves that, when peeled back, reveal a delicate, pale green heart. Other interesting lettuces are the deeply notched oak leaf types, available in red, green, and variegated colors, and crisp romaines, both red and green. Lettuce seeds can also be purchased pre-mixed in combinations called "mesclun," which also include greens and herbs such as arugula, chicory, and chervil.

Season: Sow seeds or set out transplants in early spring and late summer for late spring and fall harvests. In areas with cool summers, seeds and transplants can be planted through spring and summer as well.

Days to Harvest: Young lettuce leaves can be harvested when 3 to 4 inches long, within 3 to 4 weeks of sowing. Fully mature heads require approximately 60 days, depending upon variety.

Location: Full sun for at least three-quarters of the day.

Containers: Lettuce can be grown in containers at least 18 inches in diameter and 8 inches deep.

Germination: 3 to 7 days.

Spacing: Scatter lettuce seeds and cover lightly with soil, or rake in to about 1/4 inch deep. It is important to keep the soil moist on these shallowly planted seeds, or they will not properly germinate. Thin the seedlings to 2 to 3 inches apart if you are going to use primarily the young leaves, and to 8 inches apart if you wish to grow the heads to full maturity. The thinnings may be used in salads. Space transplants accordingly.

Growth Habit: Open-leaf, loosely packed, or tightly packed heads will form, depending upon variety.

What to Look For: The first two leaves will be slightly rounded, then the following leaves will reflect the character of the lettuce. Leaves of heading types will begin to form an increasingly large ball, while the open-leaved types will simply become larger and larger. In hot weather, the heading types may fail to form heads.

Harvest: Using scissors or a knife, cut the young leaves above their base when they are 3 to 4 inches long, and new leaves will grow in. This is called the cut-and-come-again method. The leaves may continue to be cut for several weeks or longer. To harvest full heads, cut them with a knife at their base right next to the ground.

In the Kitchen: Lettuce is eaten raw in many kinds of salads, and slipped into sandwiches, tacos, and other filled or wrapped breads. Large leaves can be used as wrappers themselves. For a main dish salad, combine lettuce with cooked chicken, hard-boiled eggs, and green onions, and dress with a vinaigrette or a creamy cheese dressing. Colorful, flavorful salads can be made using a mixture of different small garden lettuce leaves, such as red oak, green romaine, green oak, and 'Merveille de Quatre Saisons.'

It was fun when we planted a bunch of different plants. I liked when we tried the lettuce, peas, carrots, and tomatoes.

—Alexis King, first grade

Onions

(Allium cepa)

Onions are easily grown from tiny onions called sets or from transplants. They may also be started from seeds, but we recommend sets or transplants. The young sprouts are green onions or scallions. As they begin to bulb and grow, they are still green onions, although at this stage they are sometimes also referred to as spring onions. At maturity, certain varieties of onions may be dug, cured, and then put into storage.

Season: Onion sets or transplants are planted in fall and winter in areas with mild winter climates for late spring and summer harvest, and in early spring in areas with cold winters for late summer and fall harvest.

Days to Harvest: Green onions are ready for harvesting when the shoots are 10 to 12 inches tall, about 30 days after the green tips break through the earth. Full-sized onions require between 70 and 90 days to reach maturity, depending on variety and whether planted from a set or transplants. Mature onions shouldn't be harvested until more than half of the onion stalks have fallen over. They should then be dug out and left to cure for 3 days in the garden row, with the stalks covering the bulbs to prevent sunburn. Drying should continue in a well-ventilated place for another 3 weeks, and then the tops cut off, leaving a stub, and the bulbs stored, loosely packed, in a dry location.

Location: Full sun.

Containers: Onions can be grown in containers at least 12 inches across and 18 inches deep.

Germination: 10 to 14 days before shoots emerge from onion sets.

Spacing: If you are going to thin them to use some as green onions, plant both sets and transplants 1 inch apart. By the time the mature onions come along, they will be 6 inches apart. If you won't be thinning them, plant 6 inches apart.

Growth Habit: The bulb swells beneath the ground and puts forth green stalks that will eventually form blossoms on their tips, followed by seed heads.

What to Look For: Thin, green shoots appear that continue to grow and to thicken. Beneath the ground, the bulb will slowly swell. As the bulbs enlarge, their uppermost surface will be visible. Red onions will show a purplish color at the base of the stalk; yellow onions, a tinge of yellow; and white, no other coloring. The onions should be harvested before they put up a long, central seed stalk. Once this occurs, a hard core has begun to develop in the middle of the onion.

Harvest: If the ground is moist, young stalks can be pulled by hand. With slightly dry ground or bulbing onions, it is best to use a shovel. Harvesting can begin when the shoots are pencil thick and continue until the onions are mature.

In the Kitchen: Eat green or young onions raw, with or without dipping sauce; use in salads, soups, stews, and stir-fries; or grill. Slice larger onions and grill or serve raw on hamburgers. Onions can also be turned into a delicious soup or stuffed with herbed sausage and baked. Above all, onions of all types add an important seasoning element to countless dishes.

I like eating the vegetables and taking them home and cooking them. I cooked the carrots for my family. My mom helped me. We cooked them with onions and butter. They tasted really good.

—Jesslyn Jamison, third grade

Peas

(Pisum sativum)

Garden peas, also called English or shelling peas, can be consumed all along their life cycle. The young shoots can be eaten, and then later the flat young pods, sometimes called snow peas. As the peas mature and the pods become fibrous, the pods are discarded and only the peas inside—the seeds—are consumed. Sugar snap peas are a variety whose pods are sweet and edible even when mature. 'Super Sugar Mel' is a good choice for a sugar snap pea, as it is quick and easy to grow. For the French specialty petit pois, tiny supersweet peas, look for the variety 'Procovil,' which is an abundant producer.

Season: Sow seeds or set out transplants in early spring for late spring and early summer harvest, and again in mid- to late summer for a fall harvest. In areas with mild winter climates, seeds can also be sown in late fall for an early spring harvest.

Days to Harvest: Shoots can be harvested within 2 to 3 weeks after they emerge. Another 4 to 6 weeks are needed for the young pods to develop, and 1 to 2 weeks for the peas to have formed inside sufficiently for the pod to be discarded or for the edible-podded sugar snap types to mature.

Location: Full sun for at least three-quarters of the day.

Containers: Peas can be grown in containers at least 18 inches in diameter and 18 inches deep.

Germination: 5 to 8 days.

Spacing: Sow seeds 1 inch deep and 4 inches apart. Space transplants 4 inches apart.

Growth Habit: Pea plants range from dwarf bush types only 18 inches high to semivining types that may grow to 3 feet. Although supports are unnecessary, a small support can help to prevent the plant from toppling and sprawling. Trimmings from tree prunings, small trellises, or a stockade of sticks secured with twine can be used.

What to Look For: The thick necks of the pea seedlings will emerge first. Once they break through the surface and uncurl, two round leaves will unfold, followed by more leaves, and then curly tendrils will branch out. The blossoms, which are also edible, appear next and will be either white or purple. (Note: Do not confuse sweet peas with edible peas. The blossoms and all parts of the sweet pea flower, *Lathryus odoratus*, are poisonous.) As the flowers bloom, wither, and fall off, they will reveal a tiny pea pod. Within a week, the first pods may be picked and eaten whole, and in another 7 to 10 days, the larger pods can be picked and shelled, or if sugar snap peas, the pod and peas can both be eaten.

Harvest: Use scissors or clippers to harvest the pea shoots. Pick the pea pods by hand or cut them with scissors.

In the Kitchen: The young, tender shoots can be eaten raw in salads, or briefly cooked in soups, stir-fries, or sautés. Flat pods, very young shelled peas, and sugar snaps can be eaten raw or cooked briefly for adding to salads, pan juices, or stir-fries, or simply seasoned with butter and fresh herbs after removing the tips and any strings. The large, mature shelled peas require longer cooking, especially if they have become slightly hard and have begun to dry. The more mature peas have a starchy, even grainy texture, making them ideal for a slowly simmered pea soup.

It's fun to plant and to dig out plants when they're stuck inside. It's fun to dig because the dirt is soft. We planted a lot of stuff already, and we wish that it grows so we can see what it is and if it's pretty.

—Alice Concordel, first grade

Peppers

(Capsicum annuum)

Sweet peppers include common bell-shaped peppers, long, horn-shaped ones called 'Corno di Toro,' and thick-walled pimientos. All sweet peppers start out green; as they mature they sweeten and, depending upon the variety, change color to red, yellow, orange, brown, and even purple and cream.

Season: Sow seeds or set out transplants mid- through late spring when the soil is warm, for summer and fall harvest.

Days to Harvest: This depends upon variety, but the range is between 70 and 100 days.

Location: Full sun.

Containers: Sweet peppers can be grown in containers at least 18 inches across and 24 inches deep.

Germination: 6 to 10 days.

Spacing: Sow seeds $1/2$ inch deep and 4 inches apart, and thin to 8 inches apart. Space transplants 8 inches apart.

Growth Habit: Sweet peppers are bushy, branching plants that grow between 18 inches and 4 feet in height.

What to Look For: The first two leaves to emerge will be narrow and pointed, followed by leaves of the same shape and increasing size. Flowers will appear initially as tiny green balls, then small, white flowers will bloom. When they die and drop, the small, green fruits will be visible.

Harvest: Sweet peppers may be harvested when they are immature, at the green stage, or left on the plant until they have changed color and sweetened. The stems should be cut with scissors or clippers.

In the Kitchen: Eat sweet peppers raw at both the mature and the immature stage, with or without dipping sauce. Chop or slice them and add to salads, omelets, or scrambled eggs. They can also be baked into bread, used for a pizza topping, or halved or quartered, seeded, brushed with olive oil, and then grilled. Cut off the tops from whole peppers, scoop out the seeds, and stuff with rice, ground beef, sausage, or any mixture and bake in the oven.

Potatoes

(Solanum tuberosum)

Although they're often referred to as tubers, potatoes are actually swollen stem ends. They are easily grown from whole potatoes or pieces of potatoes. They have little dimples called eyes, from which sprouts will emerge to become entire plants and produce more potatoes. Dozens of varieties are available, including buttery 'Yukon Gold' and 'Yellow Finn' and blue varieties such as 'All-Blue' and 'Purple Peruvian.' The seed potatoes, as they are called, can be purchased from garden centers or through mail-order catalogs.

Season: Seed potatoes can be planted in spring, as soon as the ground can be worked, through midsummer for harvest from summer into fall. In areas with mild winter climates, they can be planted at any time of the year, with the caveat that if the ground is very cold and wet, the potatoes may rot before they sprout. Transplants are not recommended.

Days to Harvest: This depends upon the variety, but the range is between 85 and 100 days.

Location: Full sun for at least three-quarters of the day.

Containers: Potatoes may be grown quite successfully in containers at least 18 inches in diameter and at least $2^1/_2$ feet deep.

Germination: Sprouts will appear within 2 to 3 weeks of planting.

Spacing: Sow whole seed potatoes, or pieces of seed potatoes that have at least one eye, 12 inches apart. An eye should be facing upward.

Growth Habit: Potatoes grow to approximately $1^1/_2$ to 2 feet of bushy plant and need soil that has good drainage. It is important to keep the plants well watered until the blooms have dropped, although be careful not to overwater.

What to Look For: Thick, succulent, heart-shaped leaves break through the surface of the soil, followed by many more. They may vary in color somewhat, depending upon the variety. The blossoms are lavender or white with yellow centers. The potatoes develop beneath the ground in clusters on the roots. When the flowers die and drop and the plant begins to wither and dry, it is time to harvest the first potatoes.

Harvest: Using a shovel, dig around the edges of the plant and then lift up, soil and all. Some potatoes will end up in the shovel, but look for others by searching through the earth with your hands.

In the Kitchen: Prick potatoes with a fork, rub them with olive oil, and bake in a dish with fresh herbs around them. To make oven fries, slice potatoes lengthwise into 1-inch-thick wedges and put them on a baking sheet. Brush them with olive oil, sprinkle with salt and pepper, and roast them. Boil potatoes, peeled or unpeeled, in salted water, drain, add a little milk and salt and pepper, and mash or beat them to make mashed potatoes. Cube or slice potatoes for soups and stews, and grate potatoes to make hash browns and potato pancakes.

Today I saw a real mouse in the garden and it was hiding in the strawberry plant. And last week I liked to pick sunflowers. And today I ate some of the flower seeds for breakfast. I like to pick strawberries, carrots, flowers, and potatoes, and mint...oh yeah, and the string beans and beans.

—Maeve Clifford, third grade

Radishes

(Raphanus sativus)

Radishes exist in many colors and shapes, although the round red variety is the most common. Pink, purple, and white, round, olive, and carrot shaped are the predominant European short-season types, but the European winter radishes, which require a longer growing season, are usually black skinned. Asian radishes include the very large white daikon and round or cylindrical, green or scarlet-fleshed varieties. These, too, require longer growing periods than the European short-season types. All are easily grown from seed.

Season: Sow seeds of short-season radishes in early spring through mid- to late summer for harvest throughout spring and into fall. Sow seeds of long-season radishes in early to midsummer for fall harvest or, in mild winter climates, for winter harvest. Transplants are not recommended.

Days to Harvest: This depends upon variety. European radishes can be harvested young after 25 days and fully mature at 35 to 40 days. Radishes that require long growing seasons may need up to 90 days or more to mature.

Location: Full sun for at least three-quarters of the day.

Containers: Short-season radishes are easily grown in containers that are at least 12 inches in diameter and 12 inches deep. Containers are not suitable for large-rooted, long-season radishes.

Germination: 3 to 6 days.

Spacing: Sow seeds $^1/_2$ inch deep and 1 inch apart.

Growth Habit: The leaves of short-season radishes grow to 8 inches, and the mature root to between 1 and 4 inches. The long-season radishes, depending upon variety, produce leaves of up to a foot or more, and roots between 6 inches and 2 feet or more in length.

What to Look For: The first leaves are rounded and may be slightly scalloped, followed by larger leaves with serrated edges. As the leaves grow, they roughen and become lightly furry. The root develops beneath the ground.

Harvest: Young radishes can be pulled by hand, but it may be easier to use a shovel to dig large, fully mature ones. Short-season radishes quickly turn pithy and unpleasantly hot if they are left in the ground too long.

In the Kitchen: Radishes, especially the European ones, are typically eaten raw. The younger they are, the milder and more tender they will be. They are especially good thinly sliced and placed upon a piece of crusty baguette spread with butter. They can also be used whole for dipping or sliced into salads. Long-season radishes can be used in stir-fries, soups, and stews. They can also be eaten raw, but tend to have a more pungent flavor than their short-season cousins.

I like how the radishes grow so huge. The new ones get two leaves, then four leaves, and then six leaves. I like sunflowers too, because when they get rotten we can eat the seeds.

–Jennifer Simeon, first grade

Spinach

(Spinacea oleracea)

Spinach is a fast-growing green that can be eaten when the leaves are quite small, as well as when fully mature. They may be pointed and smooth, rounded, or wrinkled. 'Melody' is a particularly flavorsome variety.

Season: Sow seeds or set out transplants in early spring through summer for harvest from spring through fall. In areas with long, hot summers, spinach is best planted in early spring, then again in midsummer for a fall harvest.

Days to Harvest: Young, tender leaves may be harvested within 25 to 30 days, and fully mature leaves within 45 to 50 days.

Location: Full sun for at least three-quarters of the day.

Containers: Spinach may be grown in containers at least 18 inches in diameter and 18 inches deep.

Germination: 5 to 7 days.

Spacing: Sow seeds $^1/_2$ inch deep and $^1/_2$ inch apart, and thin to 3 inches apart, or scatter plant.

Growth Habit: Spinach grows in a semi-upright rosette to a height of 10 to 16 inches.

What to Look For: The first leaves are strappy, thin, and pointed. The leaves that follow will be characteristic of the mature plant.

Harvest: Cut the young leaves when they are 2 to 3 inches long, and new leaves will grow back, which in turn can be cut. The leaves may continue to be cut for several weeks or even longer. Small, medium, and large plants may also be cut, or the plant may be pulled by hand, root and all. Cut whole plants or young leaves to within 1 inch of ground level.

In the Kitchen: Eat raw in salads, combined with bacon and chopped hard-boiled eggs, green onions, olives, or tuna. Young spinach requires only a brief steaming or a few minutes in boiling water. Drain well and squeeze to remove excess moisture, then add lemon juice, salt, and pepper, or butter, and serve hot. Mix cooked spinach with a little béchamel sauce, place in a buttered dish, and bake to make a gratin.

Squash — Summer

(Cucurbita pepo)

Summer squashes are those that we eat when they are immature, the skin fine and the seeds barely developed. Zucchini, sometimes called Italian squash, is the best known of the summer squashes, but there are other flavorful types as well, including pattypan or scalloped squash, and yellow crookneck and straightneck. Of the many varieties of zucchini, the round French 'Ronde de Nice,' which has a pale green skin, is exceptionally delicate, as is 'Greyzini,' also with a pale green skin. 'Raven' has deep, dark green fruit and is also fine fleshed. The blossoms of summer squash are edible and have a slightly nutty flavor. The male blossoms may be harvested, or the small fruits picked with female blossoms attached.

Season: Sow seeds or set out transplants from spring to midsummer when the ground is warm, for early summer to early fall harvest.

Days to Harvest: This depends upon the variety, but most summer squash are ready to harvest in approximately 45 days.

Location: Full sun.

Containers: Summer squash can be grown in containers at least 18 inches across and 18 inches deep.

Germination: 4 to 6 days.

Spacing: Sow seeds $1/2$ inch deep and 4 inches apart, and thin to 12 inches apart. Space transplants 12 inches apart.

Growth Habit: Some of the summer squashes grow on compact bushes, while others have a more spreading habit.

What to Look For: The thick neck will burst through the soil, often with the seed case still clinging to the emerging leaves, which will be smooth and round. The next leaves will resemble those of the mature plant and may be dark green, or green mottled with silver green, and serrated. As the plant grows, fine, prickly hairs will cover the underside of the leaves and the stems. The female blossoms will be identifiable by the swelling, which, if pollinated, will become the fruit, attached to the bud; the male blossoms will be on stems with no swelling evident.

Harvest: Harvest blossoms in the morning when they are fully open. Place them in a glass of water or in a resealable plastic bag and store in the refrigerator. Use within 24 hours. To harvest baby squashes with the blossoms attached, cut from the plant when the blossom is fully open, place in a plastic bag, and store in the refrigerator. All summer squashes are most flavorful when harvested young, as the flesh deteriorates and becomes pithy and spongy around the seeds as they develop. Between 4 and 8 inches in length for long squash is a good size for harvest, while 2 to 4 inches in diameter is ideal for round types. The stems should be cut with a knife or clippers.

In the Kitchen: Young, tender squashes may be eaten raw, cut into rounds or sticks and then dipped into sauces. Grate larger squashes, mix with an egg, a little flour, salt, and pepper, and cook in a skillet or on a griddle to make savory pancakes. Squashes are also excellent steamed and dressed with a pat of butter or an herb vinaigrette. Or they may be added to soups and stews, combined in a sauté with other vegetables of the season such as tomatoes and eggplants, or baked into gratins. Because of their shape, they are good candidates for stuffing, after first being scooped out to make a shell.

I like the garden because it's really, really big, and we get to plant a lot of veggies and then eat the stuff.

—Eric Elderbrock, third grade

Squash — Winter

(Cucurbita maxima, C. mixta, C. moschata)

Winter squashes, and these include pumpkins, are those that are eaten when the seeds are mature and the skin has become hard. Because of these tough exteriors, the squashes can be stored for months in a cool, dry place. When children grow them, they are able to savor their harvest stored throughout the winter, just as our ancestors did, when there were no supermarkets to supply daily needs and winter storage vegetables were relied upon for survival. Among the many winter squash varieties that are especially fine for cooking and that have dense, meaty, flavorful flesh are the acorn, butternut, and Hubbard. Of these, some of the standard varieties are 'Acorn Table Queen,' 'Waltham Butternut,' 'Blue Hubbard,' and 'Green Hubbard.'

Pumpkins vary considerably in the quality of their meat, with some being more suitable for making jack-o'-lanterns and for Halloween display than for eating. 'New England Pie' and 'Sugar Pie' pumpkins are excellent for cooking, as are the French varieties, 'Musquée de Provence' and 'Rouge d'Etampes.'

Season: Sow seeds or set out transplants in late spring or early summer, depending upon the length of time specified for the variety you are planting, for fall harvest.

Days to Harvest: This varies greatly, depending on variety, from 120 days for 'Blue Hubbard' to 85 days for 'Jack O'Lantern' pumpkin.

Location: Full sun.

Containers: Small-sized pumpkins and other winter squashes may be grown in containers at least 18 inches in diameter and 18 inches deep.

Germination: 5 to 8 days.

Spacing: Sow seeds 1 inch deep and 12 inches apart. Thin to 2 feet apart for small-fruited types, and 3 feet apart for large-fruited ones.

Growth Habit: Most winter squashes grow on vines that reach between 6 and 15 feet long, depending on the variety. Some are bush types.

What to Look For: The first two leaves are large and may still have the seed casing attached to them as they emerge from the soil. As the plants grow and spread, deep yellow blossoms, which are edible, will appear. The early blossoms will be male. When the female blossoms appear, each one will have a distinct, very small squash attached at its base. Once pollinated, the squashes will begin to swell and grow, gradually changing color as they mature.

Harvest: Harvest when the vines have died down, the outer skin is hard, and the stems have begun to dry. Cut with a knife, leaving a length of stem. Let the squashes cure outside for a few days, then store in a cool, dry place.

In the Kitchen: Winter squash may be baked whole or in slices, or steamed, with or without the skin. Eat them simply plain, seasoned with butter, salt, pepper, and herbs, or purée and mash them and mix with other ingredients such as chopped nuts or sweet peppers. Winter squashes make excellent soups (see pages 104 and 124), or can be used to fill ravioli or pie shells, or incorporated into baked goods such as breads and cookies.

It's fun to work in the garden. I like to plant stuff – plant pumpkins, and corn. You can cut the tall corn stalks and let them dry out and then tie them up, and you can put them up for decoration on Halloween night.

—Madeleine Nelson, first grade

Strawberries

(Fragaria vesca)

Strawberries are prolific and easy to grow. Many varieties exist, some producing fruits throughout the summer and into the fall, others producing only during one period. They are typically grown from transplants rather than from seed. Since they are perennials, they will produce year after year.

Season: Set out transplants in spring through early summer. Sowing seeds is not recommended.

Days to Harvest: Most plants will start producing harvestable fruit in 45 days.

Location: Full sun for at least three-quarters of the day.

Containers: Strawberries are easily grown in containers at least 12 inches across and 18 inches deep. Strawberry jars, usually of terra-cotta, are special containers for growing strawberries, with a little pocket for each plant.

Spacing: Plant transplants 12 inches apart.

Growth Habit: Plants grow upright to about 10 inches. They put out runners that may reach out another foot or two.

What to Look For: Shiny, serrated, round leaves emerge on dormant plants first, followed by white blossoms. When the berries first appear, they are tiny and straw colored, and as they grow they turn white and eventually red when ripe.

Harvest: Cut the stems of the strawberries with clippers or scissors.

In the Kitchen: Sample strawberries fresh with no other treatment, or slice them and sprinkle with sugar or combine with other fruits for a salad. Use for making strawberry pie or strawberry jam, the latter either cooked or freezer-made (page 108).

Sunflowers

(Helianthus annuus)

Sunflowers are included here for two reasons: they can be quite easily grown and the seeds collected and stored to eat over the winter, and they are a wonderful summery element in the garden. There are a number of sunflower varieties for ornamental use and as a source for oil, but for seed harvest the large-seeded, striped confectionery types like 'Mammoth' (sometimes called 'Giant Russian') are best.

Season: Sow sunflower seeds or set out transplants after all danger of frost has passed, as sunflowers are highly susceptible to cold.

Days to Harvest: 65 to 85 days.

Location: Full sun.

Containers: The large-seeded confectionery types are not suitable for container growing because they are too large.

Germination: 5 to 7 days.

Spacing: Sow seeds 1 inch deep and 8 to 12 inches apart.

Growth Habit: Sunflowers can grow 8 to 10 feet tall, with a large seed head up to 12 inches in diameter.

What to Look For: The first leaves will be round, tapering to a point, while later leaves will be more slender with a pronounced point. A central stalk will develop and produce a bud on the tip that looks like a tight button. Gradually the bud will get larger and larger, until the green sepals open back to reveal the dark center. As the flower continues to open, the tiny flowers inside, the florets, bloom, beginning with the ray florets, each with an outsized yellow petal, around the outer edge, and then moving in a circular pattern to the centermost florets.

Harvest: When the blooms can be rubbed off the head and the seeds are hard and dry, the head can be cut and stored (see page 30).

In the Kitchen: Sunflower seeds can be salted and toasted in the oven to be eaten out of hand. The seeds can be cracked and the interior kernel added to salads, to sandwich spreads, or used in bread baking.

(Lycopersicum esculentum)

The tomato is America's favorite vegetable, and its favorite vegetable garden plant. A veritable cornucopia of tomato varieties are available to the gardener, from old-fashioned heirloom types to modern hybrids. The fruits may be red, orange, pink, yellow, white, striped, or even green, and plants may be bush or vining. Among the heirlooms, look for large beefsteak types like 'Marvel Stripe,' 'Brandywine,' 'Mortgage Lifter,' 'White Wonder,' and 'Evergreen.' Newer hybrids include yellow-and-red-striped 'Tigerelle,' a medium-sized tomato, and the slightly smaller 'Green Zebra,' which has a sweet, juicy chartreuse interior and green skin streaked with gold. All-time favorites are mid-sized 'Early Girl' and large 'Big Boy.' Of the cherry types, 'Sungold' and 'Sweet 100,' both very small, are so full of sugar they taste like candy. Determinate vines grow to a point and then stop; indeterminate vines, weather permitting, continue to grow.

Season: Sow seeds and set out transplants in late spring and into summer for summer and early fall harvest.

Days to Harvest: This depends greatly upon variety. Some mature in as little as 65 days, while others require up to 100 days.

Location: Full sun.

Containers: Bush tomatoes may be grown in containers at least 18 inches in diameter and 18 inches deep. Vining tomatoes are not suited to container growing.

Germination: 7 to 10 days.

Spacing: Sow seeds $1/4$ inch deep and 6 inches apart, and thin to 2 feet apart. Plant transplants 12 inches apart.

Growth Habit: Bush types grow to 2 feet and require little or no support. Vine types are often given support, provided by wire teepees or cylinders, by strong trellises, or by stakes and strings.

What to Look For: The first two leaves are narrow and pointed, followed by wide, serrated leaves that are generally hairy. Yellow blossoms signal the coming fruits. As the flowers are pollinated and the petals drop, the tomatoes will be apparent as small, green globes. They will grow larger and larger, turning a light green and then typically reddening as they ripen, with some color exceptions. 'White Wonder' becomes a pale ivory yellow when fully ripe, while 'Brandywine' is opalescent pink. 'Evergreen' stays green, but develops a light green cast as it ripens. 'Black Russian' and 'Russian Krim' are red only at the bottom, with the tops turning a rich forest green.

Harvest: Cut the tomato stems with clippers or hand-pick.

In the Kitchen: Slice or chop tomatoes for salads, either alone or with other vegetables and herbs. Make Italian bread salad by adding garlic-rubbed croutons to chopped tomatoes and basil, and tossing with a vinaigrette. For breakfast tomatoes, sprinkle large tomato slices with salt and pepper and cook them briefly in a nonstick pan. Prepare an easy pasta sauce by peeling a dozen large tomatoes, adding garlic, onion, salt, and pepper, and then cooking them down to half their volume. Tomatoes cooked with their summer companions—eggplants, zucchini, and sweet peppers—in olive oil and seasoned with thyme, salt, and black pepper make the classic ratatouille.

I like having corn, and beans, and tomatoes. The tomatoes I eat just like strawberries. I also like Caesar salad.

—Benjamin Hunt, third grade

Au Marché

Open markets, *les marchés*, are an old tradition in France, and along with *potagers*, are the most important sources of fresh, seasonal ingredients for the French table. Shoppers are enticed by displays that change with the season, with artfully stacked towers of leeks and radishes in spring, pyramids of tomatoes and eggplant in summer, newly dug potatoes and heaping piles of shelling beans in fall, and in winter, pumpkins and squash, with colorful flesh.

Traditionally farmers came to the market from nearby, a morning trip from the farm that was once a horse and wagon ride away but is now a brief journey by truck. At the market, shoppers know their vendors, ask questions of them, and peruse the fruits and vegetables. They know that the same seller will be there the next week, so they can discuss how the squash tasted when it was made into a gratin or soup, whether the flavor was fully developed or not. Children accompany their parents to the market, and from the earliest age are privy to the exchanges between the steward of the land and the master of the kitchen. As the adults converse, children are offered a carrot, a sweet summer peach, or a slice of perfectly ripe melon, so that they learn to appreciate the taste of fresh food.

Today, the United States is experiencing an explosive growth in farmers' markets, the equivalent of the French *marchés*. Many of the farmers are young and dedicated to growing the best-tasting fruits and vegetables possible, while using only organic farming practices. The stewardship of the land and its connection to the customers who will eat the produce is a bond that the farmers seek to build. Thus a question asked about how something is grown or how it should be cooked will be answered enthusiastically and in great detail, forging the link between the food we eat and its origin.

At farmers' markets one finds a huge, seasonal diversity that reflects the passion and interest of the grower in exploring the world of food and farming. In an effort to preserve and increase the diversity of their crops, some farmers are acquiring vegetables and fruits that are no longer readily available through commercial channels. In summertime these activities are evident, as one sees farmers with twenty to forty different kinds of tomatoes, some hybrids, some open pollinated, some new introductions, and others heirlooms. Instead of just the familiar red tomato, children can see many different colors—pink, green, and yellow striped; orange; gold; and white—in forms ranging from tiny pear shapes to flattened globes to pendulous ovals, some smooth, others lumpy. More important still, they can taste the great variety in flavors that exists in this wealth of diversity.

These farmers' markets are also occasions for experiencing a sense of community. A wonderful feeling of camaraderie ripples through the marketplace. Taking children to shop at a farmers' market informs them about the sense of community and working together that comes from supporting local businesses. From that lesson, they learn the importance of being part of a socially and economically vital community, and how that involvement contributes to one's health and well-being.

Chapter Four

Herbs: A Feast for the Senses

HERBS LEND THEIR INIMITABLE FLAVOR to food, and their fragrance and taste can elevate even humble fare to the extraordinary. But it is in the garden where the full range of their sensory virtues can be explored. They are a visual delight, with foliage in subtle shades of gray and green, flowers colored from brilliant orange to delicate mauve, and leaf patterns spiky to globular, and the fragrances of herbs are unforgettable. Picked and brought into the kitchen, fresh herbs give off their intense aroma and lure everyone to the table. For children discovering the sensory world, herb gardens are a small universe where each herb has its discrete fragrance, beauty, and taste.

In this chapter you will find profiles of twelve commonly used culinary herbs. As in the chapter on vegetables, each is annotated with growing information and a few simple kitchen ideas. Transplants are suggested for the herbs that are either difficult or time-consuming to grow from seed, while sowing seeds is recommended for the remainder. But, since even small herb transplants are redolent of fragrance, children can discover the sensory pleasure of herbs right away if they start with transplants. Also included in this chapter are plans for two little herb gardens and a collection of simple recipes using herbs. Most require no cooking, which makes them easy for even very young children to accomplish. Culinary herbs are often treated as a group, defined as garden plants that are used as secondary, not primary, ingredients in cooking. The individuals within each group, however, are highly diverse. They include annuals, perennials, and biennials that belong to a range of different genera and species, and there is likewise a diversity among their fragrances, tastes, and growth habits.

Culinary herbs may be divided into two general categories, the woody herbs and the green herbs. The former are woody-stemmed perennials that have a relatively low water content and are thus well adapted to dry conditions. The green herbs may be annuals such as basil, perennials like tarragon, or biennials like parsley, but they are all distinguished by succulent leaves and stems with a high water content, and they must be well watered to flourish and grow. Because of the different water needs, it is best to separate the two types in the garden: too much water can kill the woody herbs, while too little will decimate a planting of green herbs.

Olfaction

Odors are, together with what our eyes see, the first signals for taste. They inform us of the smell, the degree of freshness, or the extent of cooking of food or drink.

As we smell, odors are sent directly to the nasal mucous membrane. As soon as food gets into our mouth, what we experience going through the post-nasal cavity is no longer an odor but an aroma. Aromas are odors modified by the temperature within the mouth. Smell is basic to taste.

To educate taste, the nose must be put to work. Teach your child to smell all of nature's odors (woods, iodine by the seashore, cut hay, odors of the garden, of fruits, vegetables, etc.). Offer to her young nose various herbs and spices in your cooking. Finally, be understanding when she has a cold. Without smell, she cannot appreciate what she eats. The food has "no taste."

—From *Le Goût et L'Enfant (Taste and the Child)*
by Jacques Puisais

In a garden of woody herbs, spiky blue-flowered rosemary with its intense resinous mountain scent can grow next to the compact, tiny-leaved thyme that sports delicately flavored mauve flowers in springtime. Sage in all its colorful varieties is at home here, too. When it blooms, it sends forth tall spires covered with bright purple blossoms. Also suitable for this garden are marjoram, oregano, bay laurel, and lavender.

The green herbs one might find growing together in an annual herb garden are the various varieties of basil; lacy-leaved dill, which is eventually topped with umbrils of yellow flowers on long stalks; fennel, similar in appearance to dill; and cilantro. Quick-growing arugula is a favorite, and so are the round-leaved, brightly flowered nasturtiums. Here, too, is the familiar parsley, along with chives, tarragon, and mint.

A Garden of Green Herbs

A planting of both annual and perennial green herbs, which thrive in moist, rich soil, will provide an array of fragrance and flavors from spring until frost. A garden space of 5 square feet is adequate. For an immediately satisfying garden experience for children, choose all transplants, as handling the plants will give them a chance to explore the different fragrances among the herbs and to anticipate how they might be used in the kitchen once the plants have established themselves and the first snippings can be taken.

Prepare the garden site as directed on page 29 and transplant two or three of each of the following: basil, cilantro, dill, mint, and tarragon. If you are planting in containers, choose one large enough to hold at least one of each plant. Water and maintain the garden as directed on page 31, or on page 32 for container plantings. The herbs will be ready to start snipping within two or three weeks.

A Garden of Woody Herbs

Planting an herb garden of woody perennials—thyme, sage, rosemary, and marjoram—will ensure the kitchen a nearly year-round supply of resinous herbs to season grilled meats and vegetables, sauces, soups, stews, oils, and vinegars with the flavors of the Mediterranean, where these herbs grow wild. A garden space of 5 square feet is adequate. As in the green herbs garden, transplants are recommended because children can enter into the gardening experience immediately with a sensory exploration of the herbs they are planting, rubbing leaves between their fingers to release the fragrance, and imagining what foods they might season. Additionally, all of these herbs are either slow or irregular to grow from seed.

Prepare the garden site as directed on page 29, and transplant two each of the following: thyme, sage, rosemary, and marjoram. If you are planting in containers, choose one large enough to hold at least one of each plant. Water and maintain the garden as directed on page 31, or on page 32 for container plantings, remembering that the woody herbs require far less water than the green herbs.

Arugula

(Eruca sativa)

Arugula, also called rocket and roquette, is a quick-growing annual whose succulent green leaves are nutty when young, becoming distinctively spicy as they grow and mature. The dainty white blossoms are edible, too.

Season: Sow seeds in spring through early fall for harvest throughout spring until frost. Transplants are not recommended because arugula is so easily grown from seed.

Days to Harvest: Young arugula can be cut in about 20 days from sowing, and large, mature leaves in 35 to 40 days.

Location: Full sun.

Containers: Arugula is easily grown in containers at least 8 inches in diameter and 8 inches deep.

Germination: 3 to 5 days.

Spacing: Sow seeds $1/4$ inch deep and 1 inch apart, and thin to 3 inches apart, or scatter plant, thinning as desired.

Growth Habit: Plants grow in a rosette form, and will become bushy and branching, reaching 2 feet.

What to Look For: The first 4 to 6 leaves are bright green, smooth, spoon shaped, and 3 to 4 inches long. The next leaves are notched at the bottom and slightly larger. As the plant continues to grow and mature, the leaves will become dark green, 6 to 8 inches long, and heavily notched along their length.

Harvest: Cut arugula leaves with scissors or a knife, or pull up the entire plant.

In the Kitchen: Use young arugula in salads on its own or mixed with other lettuces. Make a bed of arugula leaves and top with warm chicken, fish such as salmon or halibut, or with seared steak or grilled game bird. Combine arugula with sweet fruits and salty cheese, oranges and feta, for example. Add it to sandwiches, burritos, tacos, or hamburgers. Cook mature leaves to add to pasta filling mixtures or to toss with pasta.

Basil

(Ocimum basilicum)

There are a number of different varieties of basil, a popular annual, but the most common are large-leaved Italian, also called sweet basil, and purple basil, with the latter having a slightly more pungent overlay to the spiced perfume taste that we have come to associate with the herb. Less common are the flavored basils, like lemon and anise; Thai basil, also know as Asian basil; and small-leaved or globe basil.

Season: Sow seeds or set out transplants in late spring and early summer when the ground is warm for harvest through summer until frost.

Days to Harvest: Basil can be cut in about 45 days from sowing, and earlier from transplants.

Location: Full sun.

Containers: All types of basil may be grown in containers at least 8 inches in diameter and 8 inches deep.

Germination: 5 to 7 days.

Spacing: Sow seeds $1/2$ inch deep and 1 inch apart, and thin to 4 inches apart. Space transplants 4 inches apart.

Growth Habit: Bushy plants may grow to 2 feet.

What to Look For: The first leaves are nearly triangular, while the following leaves take the characteristic shape of the mature foliage. Several stalks grow from the base of the plant, and each puts up a seed head, initially as a spiky cluster of white or lavender blossoms. These should be cut back to encourage leafy growth.

Harvest: Cut basil sprigs with scissors or clippers just above any leaf. New growth will appear. As the plants continue to grow and mature, their flavor will intensify and become hot, even bitter, especially in sizzling weather. The fresh new growth will be milder.

In the Kitchen: Use basil to make pesto, and to season summer vegetables. For an easy summer salad, slice tomatoes and fresh mozzarella, and arrange on a platter with whole basil leaves. Drizzle with olive oil and sprinkle with salt and pepper.

Chives

(Allium schoenoprasum)

Chives, or common chives as they are sometimes called, are a perennial with a mild onionlike flavor. Garlic chives have flat rather than tubular leaves and taste of garlic. Transplants are recommended in both cases.

Season: Set out transplants in spring through early summer for harvest until frost.

Days to Harvest: Chives may be harvested as soon as they produce a dozen or so new shoots.

Location: At least 6 hours of full sun.

Containers: Chives can be grown in containers that are at least 6 inches in diameter and 6 inches deep.

Germination: 7 to 10 days.

Spacing: Space transplants 6 inches apart.

Growth Habit: Clumping plants grow to 1 foot and have flower spikes of equal length when in bloom.

What to Look For: Leaves are narrow and tubular with pointed tips. The flowers will first appear as tight buds, then will open to rosy lavender flowers. The buds and flowers are edible as well.

Harvest: Snip chives with scissors. Harvest flowers before they are fully open, as they become fibrous and papery as they mature.

In the Kitchen: Use chives, their buds, and their blossoms to flavor egg and potato dishes of all kinds and to add to soups, stews, salads, and salad dressings. Use chives to season tomatoes and cucumbers and to make flavored butters and cheeses.

Cilantro

(Coriandrum sativum)

Cilantro, also called fresh coriander or Chinese parsley, is an annual with a cool, refreshing, nearly perfumed flavor. It is used extensively in Mexican and Asian cooking.

Season: Sow seeds or set out transplants in early spring through mid-summer for summer and fall harvest.

Days to Harvest: Plan on 45 days for first clippings, 65 days for mature plants.

Location: Full sun for three-quarters of the day.

Containers: Cilantro can be grown in containers at least 8 inches in diameter and 6 inches deep.

Germination: 7 to 10 days.

Spacing: Sow seeds 1 inch deep and 2 inches apart, and thin to 4 inches apart. Space transplants 4 inches apart.

Growth Habit: Bushy plants grow to between 12 and 18 inches.

What to Look For: The first leaves are round with serrated edges, followed by more of the same, growing on increasingly long stems. When the plant starts to flower, the leaves become elongated, tightly grouped, and feathery, altogether different than the early foliage.

Harvest: Begin harvesting after plants reach about 8 inches tall.

In the Kitchen: Cilantro seasons corn, tomatoes, chiles, cucumbers, and onions. It goes well with meats and fish, and is used in soups and salsas. For a salsa to accompany tacos or chips, chop tomatoes, onions, and cilantro and add a little salt and pepper. The tiny, white flowers are edible and, along with the intensely flavored roots, can be used for seasoning as well.

Dill

(Anethum graveolens)

Dill, an annual, is used in both the leafy green stage, when it is sometimes called baby dill, and in the mature stage, when it is topped with a spreading yellow seed head.

Season: Sow seeds in spring and into midsummer for summer and fall harvest.

Days to Harvest: Plan on 45 to 50 days for young dill, and 65 to 75 days for seed heads.

Location: Full sun for at least three-quarters of the day.

Containers: For early cutting, but not for mature seed heads, dill can be successfully grown in containers at least 8 inches in diameter and 12 inches deep.

Germination: 10 to 14 days.

Spacing: Sow seeds $1/4$ inch deep and 1 to 2 inches apart, and thin to 5 inches apart. Plant transplants 5 inches apart.

Growth Habit: Dill grows to 4 feet on large-stalked, branching plants with feathery leaves.

What to Look For: The first leaves are very fine and lacy. As the plant grows, it puts up a central stalk that produces branches of airy, feathery leaves. Eventually the stalks bloom with yellow flowers, which become broad seed heads.

Harvest: Cut the young dill with scissors or clippers. The plant will continue to produce new growth. Cut the stalk with clippers or a knife to harvest the seed heads.

In the Kitchen: Mix chopped dill into yogurt to make a dip for raw vegetables, or add it to potato or cucumber salads. Add chopped dill to melted butter for pouring over boiled potatoes or steamed carrots. The seed heads are generally used as a pickling spice.

Marjoram

(Origanum marjorana)

A perennial in all but cold winter climates, marjoram is closely related to oregano, which it resembles, although the former has a smaller leaf and a slightly milder, yet still resinous, flavor. Its fragrance is sharp and pungent, and it is commonly used in Italian and Greek cooking. Transplants are recommended.

Season: Set out transplants in spring through early summer for harvest until frost.

Days to Harvest: Harvest may start as soon as there are 2 inches of new growth.

Location: Full sun.

Containers: Marjoram can be grown in containers at least 8 inches in diameter and 8 inches deep.

Spacing: Plant transplants 6 inches apart.

Growth Habit: Bushy plants grow to 2 feet, and when in bloom have flower spikes up to 1 foot long.

What to Look For: Leaves are slightly triangular and somewhat fuzzy. When the plant begins to flower, spikes will be covered with pale green clusters of buds that will bloom into white flowers. The buds and flowers are edible. To encourage leafy growth, however, the flower spikes should be cut back.

Harvest: Cut marjoram sprigs with scissors or clippers. New growth will appear.

In the Kitchen: Use marjoram to flavor tomato sauces, pizzas, chicken, and vegetables of all kinds, especially those associated with the Mediterranean kitchen, such as eggplant, zucchini, and sweet peppers.

Mint

(Mentha peperita)

Peppermint (Mentha peperita) *is one of the many different mints, all of which are perennials, that are available. Each has its own distinct flavor and heady aroma. Lemon mint, spearmint, and orange mint are among the more commonly found varieties. Transplants are recommended.*

Season: Set out transplants in spring through summer for harvest until frost.

Days to Harvest: Harvest may start as soon as there are 2 inches of new growth.

Location: Partial shade, with at least 4 hours of sun.

Containers: Mint can be grown in containers at least 8 inches in diameter and 8 inches deep.

Spacing: Plant transplants 6 inches apart.

Growth Habit: Spreading bushes grow to between 10 inches and 2 feet tall.

What to Look For: Leaves vary somewhat from round to elongated, with delicately serrated edges. The fully white flower heads should be cut back to encourage leafy growth.

Harvest: Snip mint sprigs with scissors or clippers.

In the Kitchen: Mix whole leaves into drinks, such as lemonade, tea, or sodas. Add chopped fresh mint leaves to salads and yogurt, and use as a topping for split-pea soup, lamb stew, and rice pilaf.

Nasturtium

(Tropaeolum majus and minus)

Although today they are usually thought of as flowers, nasturtiums have been a favorite edible green in the United States and Europe for more than a century, with both leaves and blossoms delivering their peppery taste to salads. Bush, vining, and semivining varieties exist, with the flowers in many different colors, but for culinary purposes, they are all equal.

Season: Sow seeds in late spring and into summer when the ground is warm. They will grow quickly and can be harvested until the first frost. Seeds may also be planted in late summer for a fall harvest. Transplants are not recommended.

Days to Harvest: The first leaves are ready to harvest within 30 days. Blossoms appear 2 to 3 weeks later.

Location: Full sun for at least three-quarters of the day.

Containers: All types of nasturtiums can be grown in containers that are at least 12 inches in diameter and 12 inches deep.

Germination: 5 to 7 days.

Spacing: Sow seeds 1 inch deep and 4 inches apart for bush types, and 8 inches apart for vining types.

Growth Habit: Bush types grow to approximately 18 inches tall, while vining types can trail up to 12 feet. The latter may be given supports to climb on, such as strings, a fence, or a teepee made of sticks or other material, or they can be left simply to spread across the ground.

What to Look For: The first two leaves are distinctly round and veined. These are followed by increasingly larger leaves of similar shape, on long, succulent stems, and lastly by plump flower buds, opening to blossoms. When the flowers die, a little rumpled seedpod, also edible, forms.

Harvest: Pinch off flowers and leaves, or use scissors.

In the Kitchen: Use the leaves in salads and on sandwiches. To make a delicate, peppery butter, flecked with bright color, finely mince nasturtium blossoms and mix them into softened butter. Roll the butter into a log shape or press it into tiny bowls, cover, and refrigerate.

(Petroselinum crispum)

Parsley, which is a biennial, comes in two basic types, flat-leaf and curly. Generally the flat-leaved variety, also called Italian parsley, has the stronger flavor.

Season: Sow seeds or set out transplants in early spring through mid-summer for summer and fall harvest. In areas with mild winter climates, seeds may be sown in late fall for spring harvest, and transplants can be set out in late summer for fall and winter harvest.

Days to Harvest: About 75 days from sowing, or 1 to 2 weeks if transplanted.

Location: Full sun for at least three-quarters of the day.

Containers: Parsley can easily be grown in containers at least 6 inches deep and 6 inches in diameter.

Germination: 14 to 21 days.

Spacing: Sow seeds $1/4$ inch deep and $1/2$ inch apart, and thin to 4 inches apart. Space transplants 4 inches apart.

Growth Habit: Parsley is a bushy plant that grows to between 10 and 18 inches tall, depending upon variety.

What to Look For: The first leaves are slightly pointed, with the following leaves either serrated and flat or curly, depending upon variety, growing on long stems.

Harvest: Using scissors or clippers, start cutting parsley stems when they are 6 to 8 inches tall and new growth will continuously recur.

In the Kitchen: Parsley is an all-purpose seasoning and can be used as a base for a soup, salad, or sauce. It can also be treated as a green, just as one would spinach. For an easy and powerfully flavored salad, combine half parsley and half lettuce and dress with a lemon vinaigrette. Partner parsley with potatoes for soup, or with cheese for a tart filling, or use for flavoring pancake batter, omelets, and hash browns.

(Rosmarinus officinalis)

There are a number of different varieties of rosemary, a perennial. Some, such as 'Tuscan Blue,' are tall, with thick, upright spikes. Others, such as 'Lockwood de Forest' and 'Prostratus,' are low growing. All tolerate poor soil, as long as it is well drained. Rosemary's powerful, resinous pungency is a welcome seasoning in Mediterranean kitchens, a region where the herb thrives. Transplants are recommended.

Season: Set out transplants in early spring for year-round harvest, except in areas where winter temperatures drop below 15°. There, rosemary plants may be treated as annuals, or protected from freezing over the winter.

Days to Harvest: Harvest may start as soon as there are 2 inches of new growth.

Location: At least 6 hours of full sun.

Containers: Rosemary can be grown in containers at least 10 inches in diameter and 12 inches deep, with larger types requiring larger containers.

Spacing: Plant transplants 12 inches apart.

Growth Habit: This depends upon the variety. Some form spreading prostrate plants, while others are semispreading, and still others are upright. The flowers are blue, although a few varieties have pink flowers.

What to Look For: The leaves are thin and spiky, with new growth being more supple and less woody than the older growth.

Harvest: Snip sprigs with scissors or clippers. New growth will occur.

In the Kitchen: Use rosemary to season meats, vegetables, breads, soups, and stews. Rosemary complements grilled food: either rub the meat or vegetables all over with the herb just before putting them over the fire, or marinate them with the herb beforehand.

Sage

(Salvia officinalis)

Although there are many varieties of sage, which is a perennial, the one most commonly used in cooking is common sage. Colorful varieties to look for are 'Golden Sage' and 'Purple Sage.' Culinarily their flavor is somewhat sharper than common sage, but they are certainly beautiful in the garden. Transplants are recommended.

Season: Set out transplants in spring when danger of frost has passed for harvest until frost.

Days to Harvest: Harvest may start as soon as there are 2 inches of new growth.

Location: Full sun.

Containers: Sage can easily be grown in containers at least 12 inches deep and 8 inches in diameter.

Spacing: Plant transplants 1 foot apart.

Growth Habit: Sage is a spreading shrubby bush that can reach 2 feet. Flowers bloom on spikes that grow 1 foot above the plant.

What to Look For: The new growth on sage is often a deeper, brighter green than the older growth, which displays the characteristic gray-green color. On close inspection, the leaves themselves have a pebbled surface. The onset of flowering is noticeable by the development of large, plump, pointed buds, which are silvery. They open into purple blossoms. The buds and blossoms are edible.

Harvest: Snip sprigs with scissors or clippers.

In the Kitchen: Use sage in combination with pork chops, game birds, roasted vegetables, and in stuffings.

Tarragon

(Artemesia dracunculus)

French tarragon, also known as true tarragon, is the tarragon whose enticing citruslike flavor is used by cooks. This perennial is propagated only from cuttings, not from seed, unlike Russian tarragon, which can be grown from seed but whose flavor is inferior.

Season: Set out transplants in spring for harvest until frost.

Days to Harvest: Harvest may start as soon as there are 2 inches of new growth.

Location: Full sun.

Containers: Tarragon is easily grown in containers at least 8 inches deep and 8 inches in diameter.

Spacing: Plant transplants 1 foot apart.

Growth Habit: The plants develop into a mounded shape.

What to Look For: Leaves 1 inch long multiply on stems that may be a foot or more in length. Tender new growth will be a brighter green and the stems more supple than that of the older growth.

Harvest: Cut tarragon with scissors or clippers.

In the Kitchen: Tarragon is a classic accompaniment to fish, especially salmon and trout. It can be added to salads and used to flavor potato, pea, tomato, or bean soup. It can be added to white, brown, or cheese sauce, and used to flavor vinegar.

Thyme

(Thymus vulgaris)

There are many varieties of thyme, including an aromatic lemon-flavored plant, although common thyme is the one most typically used in the kitchen. It has a woodsy, resinous fragrance and delicately flavored blossoms that are edible as well. Transplants are recommended.

Season: Set out transplants from early spring through summer for harvest in summer and fall. In areas that are not subject to heavy freezes, thyme is a perennial and can be cut continuously.

Days to Harvest: Harvest may start as soon as there are 2 inches of new growth.

Location: Full sun for at least three-quarters of the day.

Containers: Thyme can be grown in containers at least 8 inches in diameter and 8 inches deep.

Spacing: Place transplants 8 inches apart.

Growth Habit: Thyme is a low-growing, bushy plant, reaching and spreading to 12 inches high and across.

What to Look For: As the plant continues to grow, it will produce fragrant lavender or whitish blossoms that are edible. To encourage leafy growth, keep the flowers cut back.

Harvest: Cut thyme as soon as the transplants have 2 inches of new growth, using scissors or clippers. New growth may appear lighter green than the older growth and have more supple stems.

In the Kitchen: Thyme is an important seasoning in Mediterranean cooking and is used with all meats and poultry, in baked and grilled dishes built on cheese and vegetables, and even with figs and strawberries.

Cream Cheese with Chives

Fresh herbs, in this case chives, are easily mixed into soft cheeses to flavor them. Other green herbs such as dill, basil, or nasturtium blossoms are also good choices. Freshly ground black pepper, cumin, or chile can be added for a spicy accent. Spread the cheese onto crackers or bread, or use as a dip for raw vegetables such as carrot sticks, pieces of sweet pepper, or cauliflower florets.

1 cup cream cheese, at room temperature

$^1/_2$ cup minced fresh chives

1 tablespoon milk (optional)

Put the cream cheese in a bowl and add the chives. Using a wooden spoon or a fork, mix together until the chives are evenly distributed. If necessary, add the milk to thin the mixture.

MAKES ABOUT 1 CUP

Tarragon Mustard

The addition of fresh herbs is an easy way to personalize mustard, and the resulting blend makes a nice gift. The amounts given here can be increased proportionately as desired. Other herbs to consider for flavoring are parsley, basil, and dill. Add the mustard to scrambled eggs, use on hot dogs or sandwiches, or serve as an accompaniment to grilled pork chops or sausages.

$1/4$ cup Dijon or other French-style mustard

2 tablespoons minced fresh tarragon

Put the mustard in a bowl and stir in the tarragon with a spoon.

MAKES ABOUT 1/4 CUP

Herb Mayonnaise

This is a simple exercise in sampling the flavors of different herbs. Children can prepare this quartet of mayonnaises on their own, with adult supervision as sharp knives are needed to mince the herbs. Use the mayonnaise in sandwiches or serve with artichokes or potatoes.

1¹/₂ cups mayonnaise

1 tablespoon fresh lemon juice

3 tablespoons minced fresh chives

3 tablespoons minced fresh basil

3 tablespoons minced fresh tarragon

3 tablespoons minced fresh flat-leaf parsley

Mix the mayonnaise and lemon juice thoroughly. Divide the mixture evenly among 4 small bowls. Add 1 herb to each bowl. Mix well, using a clean fork for each bowl. Serve immediately, or cover and refrigerate to use later.

MAKES 1 CUP

Mint Tea

This is actually an herbal infusion, as it is made only from mint itself and no true tea is included. Fresh mint leaves may also be added to any kind of tea as it steeps, to give a hint of mint to the poured cup.

1 cup fresh mint leaves

2 cups water

Sugar or honey to taste

Put the mint in a saucepan with the water and bring to a boil. Reduce the heat to low and simmer, uncovered, for 5 to 10 minutes, or until the water has taken on a deep greenish brown hue and tastes of mint. Strain into a teapot or cups, and serve hot with sugar and honey.

MAKES ABOUT 2 CUPS; SERVES 2 TO 4

Cilantro Butter

Herb butters are flavorful, attractive, and versatile. Numerous herbs can be used, both green and woody. The woody herbs should be mixed in sparingly, however, adding only half the amount one uses of green herbs such as the cilantro suggested here. Nasturtium butter, made from the flowers, is especially festive looking. Add flavored butter to quesadillas, scrambled eggs, or grilled vegetables, or use as a spread on toasted tomato sandwiches.

4 tablespoons butter, at room temperature

2 tablespoons minced cilantro

Put the softened butter in a bowl and add the cilantro. Using a wooden spoon or a fork, mix together until the cilantro is evenly distributed. Pack the flavored butter into a small dish or cup.

MAKES ABOUT ¼ CUP

Mint Lemonade

The addition of fresh mint gives lemonade a tangy, refreshing flavor, as well as an attractive appearance.

$^1/_4$ cup fresh mint leaves

4 cups homemade or prepared lemonade

Mint sprigs, for garnish

Add the mint leaves to the lemonade and refrigerate for 4 to 5 hours to allow the flavors to blend. When ready to serve, remove the mint leaves, pour the lemonade into tall glasses with ice, and garnish each with a mint sprig.

MAKES FOUR 1-CUP SERVINGS

Thyme Blossom Infusion

Thyme blossoms have a delicate thyme flavor and are much used in Provence for making infusions, which are then flavored with honey.

$1/2$ cup fresh thyme blossoms

1 cup boiling water

Sugar or honey to taste

Put the thyme blossoms into a saucepan and add the water. Bring to a boil, reduce the heat to low, and simmer, uncovered, for 5 to 10 minutes, or until the water has taken on a greenish brown hue. The longer the cooking time, the stronger the infusion. Strain and pour into a teapot or cups, and serve hot with sugar or honey.

MAKES ABOUT 1 CUP; SERVES 1 OR 2

Lemon Oil

Making flavored oil is a simple kitchen project in which even the youngest children can participate, and the tasty, attractive results become wonderful gifts from the garden. The familiar fragrance of lemons combines well with the strong, earthy taste of fresh thyme. For a play on flavors, try using lemon thyme.

> 3 or 4 dehydrated lemon slices
>
> 3 or 4 sprigs fresh thyme
>
> 5 to 10 peppercorns
>
> 1 quart olive oil

Using a skewer, gently slide the lemon slices and thyme into a sterilized 1-quart bottle or jar. Add the peppercorns and cover with the olive oil to within 1/2 inch of the top of the jar. Cork and let infuse in a warm place out of direct sunlight for 1 week. Store in a cupboard, where it will keep for several months.

MAKES 1 QUART

Nasturtium and Peppercorn Vinegar

Nasturtiums are prized in French gardens and potagers for their peppery flavor. Here they are used to infuse vinegar with an intense orange color and piquant taste. Use this vinegar to make marinades, deglazing sauces, or vinaigrettes.

8 to 10 fresh nasturtium blossoms

20 peppercorns

1 quart white wine or champagne vinegar

Using a wooden skewer, gently slide the blossoms into a sterilized 1-quart bottle or jar. Add the peppercorns and fill the bottle with vinegar to within $1/2$ inch of the top. Cork the top and place the bottle in a light, sunny place for at least 1 week to allow the flavors to blend. Taste the vinegar after 1 week. If it is nicely flavored, you can begin using it, or you can decorate it for giving as a gift. It it needs more time, return it to its sunny location for a few days. Once the vinegar is flavored, it will keep in the refrigerator for 2 to 3 months.

MAKES 1 QUART

CHAPTER FIVE

Seasonal Gardens with Recipes

$\mathcal{J}$N THIS CHAPTER WE MAKE SUGGESTIONS for four kitchen gardens, each accompanied by recipes that draw upon the seasonal harvest. A brief introduction to each garden includes ideas on how children can participate in the planting, and how to use the harvest in ways other than in the recipes that follow the plan.

Although each of the plans contains specific measurements and a specific number of plants, the gardens can be made smaller or larger, and include more vegetables or fewer. The information is meant to encourage the planting of a garden and the cooking of its harvest, and to suggest ways in which to teach children about seasonality in cooking.

The directions for planting, maintaining, and harvesting all the vegetables in the gardens are in Chapter 3, while activities such as drying tomatoes, collecting sunflower seeds, and drying beans are included in this chapter.

Spring Snacking Garden
Radishes, Peas, Carrots, and Parsley

This little garden can be grown in containers as well as in the ground, and is a good choice for children of all ages, as the vegetables can be snacked on raw in the garden or, once harvested, anytime. The younger ones can easily handle the large radish and pea seeds on their own, and with help can scatter the carrot seeds. The parsley should be grown from transplanted seedlings, another activ-

Making Trellises

Trellises can be constructed from many types of materials, from bamboo poles, wooden stakes, or sturdy twigs to heavy wire or metal rods.

To make a simple bamboo teepee trellis suitable for such climbers as beans, nasturtiums, peas, and morning glories, choose three lengths of bamboo, each about 1 inch in diameter and 6 feet long. Sink the poles into the soil about 8 inches deep, positioning them in a circle at equal distance from one another and slanting them slightly inward. Cross the upper ends over one another, and tie them together tightly with coarse string, to create a "tent formation." As the plants grow, they will naturally climb the structure.

ity that small children can accomplish on their own. They can use a little trowel or a "garden spoon" to dig a hole and then lower the seedling into it, after having first soaked it in a bucket of water. Older children, once they have had some assistance from adults in preparing the ground, can lay out the rows and do the planting on their own. Parents or teachers should check now and again that the children are planting neither too deeply nor too shallowly, as either may result in poor or no germination.

The garden plot will need to be $5^1/2$ feet square. Prepare the garden site as directed on page 29. Divide it into four beds, each 2 feet by 2 feet, with a $1^1/2$-foot-wide walkway between the beds. Plant the radishes, peas, and carrots as directed in Chapter 3, planting one bed of radishes, two beds of peas, and three-quarters of a bed of carrots. Transplant two or three parsley plants, equally spaced, into the remaining area. Water and maintain the garden as directed on page 31. The radishes and pea shoots will be ready for harvest first, followed by the pea pods, and later the carrots. The parsley may be harvested once it shows two inches of new growth.

If you are planting in containers, you will need at least four in the dimensions recommended for each vegetable (see Chapter 3), one for the radishes, one for the carrots, one for the peas, and one for the parsley. You will have fewer plants than if you plant in the suggested garden site, but enough to experience a good harvest. Follow the directions for preparation and maintenance of a container garden on page 32, and plant the vegetables as directed in Chapter 3.

Two simple recipes that feature these "snacking" vegetables follow, but this springtime harvest has many other uses as well. A few clippings of young pea shoots, chopped or grated carrot, or snippets of fresh parsley can be incorporated into a lettuce, potato, or pasta salad. These are easy additions that even small children can make, cutting parsley and pea shoots with blunt-nosed scissors and adding them to the final dish. The pea pods and the shoots can be added to any stir-fry, and the parsley can easily end up in any soup, stew, or sautéed dish.

Radish and Pea Pod Tray
with Parsley-Lemon Dip

This dip may also be made with cilantro or dill and any raw vegetables, such as sweet peppers, carrots, green onions, young tender pea pods of any kind, or cucumbers. Young children can be in charge of pulling up the radishes and picking the peas and, with guidance, can prepare the dip. Older children can assemble the dish on their own.

8 to 10 radishes

10 to 12 pea pods

4 or 5 sprigs parsley, chopped

$^3/_4$ cup plain yogurt

$^1/_2$ teaspoon salt

1 teaspoon freshly ground black pepper

1 tablespoon freshly squeezed lemon juice

Remove any large or damaged leaves from each radish, but leave the small ones intact, and clip off the dangling root end. Arrange the trimmed radishes in a circle on a plate. Remove any strings from the pea pods and arrange the pods on the tray with the radishes. In a bowl, mix together the parsley, yogurt, salt, pepper, and lemon juice with a spoon. Taste and adjust the seasonings; the mixture should be tangy and flecked with green. Transfer the yogurt sauce to a small serving bowl and place it on the platter with the radishes and peas.

SERVES 2 OR 3

Carrots with Parsley Sauce

The simple sauce of fresh minced parsley and butter can be used for other vegetables, such as new potatoes, green beans, peas, and spinach. Snipping parsley with blunt scissors is a good job for a small child, who can also finish the dish by adding the butter and parsley.

> **6 carrots**
>
> **4 cups water**
>
> **1 teaspoon salt**
>
> **2 tablespoons unsalted butter**
>
> **10 to 12 sprigs parsley, chopped**
>
> **$^1/_2$ teaspoon freshly ground black pepper**

Trim the carrots and discard or compost the green tops. Cut the carrots crosswise into $^1/_2$-inch-thick slices. Place them in a saucepan with the water and $^1/_2$ teaspoon of the salt. Cover and bring to a boil over medium-high heat. Reduce the heat to low and simmer, covered, until the carrots can easily be pierced with the tines of a fork, about 15 minutes. Drain the carrots and return them to the saucepan. Add the butter and parsley and place over low heat. Cook just until the butter has melted, about 1 minute. Season with the remaining salt and pepper and serve hot.

SERVES 3 OR 4

Summer Salad Garden
Tomatoes, Corn, Beans, Cucumbers, Dill, Cilantro, and Basil

In this garden, children can be in charge of soaking the seedlings and digging holes for them, or sowing the seeds. The herb seeds may be scatter planted by even the youngest child. A planting of approximately six tomato plants, twenty-four corn stalks, a dozen bean plants, four cucumber vines, and a half dozen each of cilantro, dill, and basil will keep salads on the table all summer long.

Prepare the garden site as directed, on page 29. You will need a garden plot of about 120 square feet, divided into eight beds, each about 1 foot wide and 6 feet long, with a $1^{1}/_{2}$-foot-wide path along one side of each bed. Plant the corn, tomatoes, beans, dill, cilantro, basil, and cucumber as directed in Chapter 3, planting four rows of corn, one row of tomatoes, one row of cucumbers, one of beans, and one row with all the herbs—dill, cilantro, and basil. Be sure to plant the corn to the north or east where it won't shade out the smaller plants as it grows, or if you have the space, put it in a separate location.

The tomatoes, beans, and herbs can be easily grown in containers. The cucumbers can, too, but you will need to supply a trellis to support them. Corn, however, is difficult to grow in a container.

Planted at the same time, from seed or from transplants, the vegetables will all be ready for harvest at nearly the same time. The ears of corn, depending upon variety, will produce during a three- to four-week period, but all the other vegetables and the herbs will continue to produce throughout the summer.

Although recipes for two summery salads follow, many other combinations are possible, including those that might incorporate grains, pasta, meat, fish, or chicken, as well as lettuces and other greens. Of course, the vegetables of a summer salad garden aren't relegated solely to the salad bowl. Boiled or grilled corn slathered with butter and sprinkled with chopped cilantro or basil, pasta with a quick tomato and herb sauce, green beans stir-fried with corn, and summer soups can all be made from the garden's harvest.

A First Sprout Party

It is helpful, especially with small children, to have events that mark a garden's progress. It encourages them to keep involved and interested in the growing process from seed to harvest, which can seem like a long time to a child. One way to do this is to have a little party to celebrate the first sprout, just as harvest parties are traditional celebrations in the adult community. Draw and color invitations, depicting and labeling the newly emerged sprout. At the party, go out into the garden to view the sprouts, then come up with games that bring the garden to the party. For example, you might suggest playing pin the root on the carrot top, or the seed head on the sunflower stalk.

Corn, Rice, and Tomato Salad
with Basil

Although this salad requires several steps, all are easy, and this colorful and festive dish can be assembled quickly. The smoky flavor of the corn gives the resulting combination an appealing outdoor flavor, and children enjoy peeling back the charred husks to reveal the cooked corn. An adult should remove the kernels from the cob, however, as a sharp knife and a hard stroke are required. Older children can chop the tomatoes, and children of any age will enjoy mixing the ingredients together.

$^1/_2$ teaspoon salt

1 teaspoon freshly ground black pepper

$^1/_4$ cup red wine vinegar

6 tablespoons fruity cold-pressed olive oil

2 cups cooked long-grain white rice, at room temperature

4 ears of corn, in their husks

2 or 3 tomatoes

$^1/_4$ cup chopped basil, plus extra leaves for garnish

Prepare a charcoal fire. Combine the salt, pepper, vinegar, and olive oil together in the bottom of a bowl large enough to hold all the ingredients eventually. Add the rice, and, using a fork, separate the grains. Set aside.

Put a grill rack over the fire, and place the corn, still in its husks, on the rack. Cook 4 to 5 minutes, until the husks are charred and when peeled back show the color of the corn has begun to change. Turn and cook another 4 to 5 minutes, until peeling back the husks reveals the corn has changed color on the second side. Remove from the grill and let cool. While the corn is cooling, chop the tomatoes into $1/2$-inch pieces. Drain them in a sieve and then add them to the rice mixture, stirring them in with the fork. Strip off the husks and silks from the ears of corn. Using a sharp knife, cut the corn kernels off each cob and stir them into the rice mixture along with the chopped basil. Cover and refrigerate for 1 hour to allow the flavors to blend. Taste and adjust the seasonings with salt and pepper. Garnish with basil leaves and serve slightly chilled or at room temperature.

SERVES 4 TO 6

Tomato and Cucumber Platter
with Fresh Dill

This salad platter could also incorporate slices of sweet pepper and crumbled feta cheese. Basil or cilantro can be used instead of the dill. Young children can arrange the tomato and cucumber slices on the platter, and use blunt-nosed scissors to snip the dill. Older children, if adept with a knife, can make this dish on their own.

4 tomatoes, thinly sliced

3 cucumbers, peeled and thinly sliced

$^1/_4$ cup chopped dill

$^1/_2$ teaspoon salt

1 teaspoon freshly ground black pepper

$^1/_4$ to $^1/_3$ cup unseasoned rice wine vinegar

To assemble the platter, alternate each tomato slice with a cucumber slice, or make a row of tomato slices, and then one of cucumber slices. Sprinkle the dill, salt, and pepper over the arranged slices, and drizzle the vinegar evenly over the vegetables, adjusting the amount to taste. Serve immediately, or cover and refrigerate for up to 3 hours before serving to allow the flavors to blend.

SERVES 4 TO 6

Fall Soup Garden
Beans, Pumpkins, Spinach, Tomatoes, and Potatoes

Pumpkins hold a fascination for children, who are delighted by the idea of planting them because there is a clear image of what will eventually appear in the garden. The large pumpkin seeds are easy to sow, as are those of beans, which are also included in this garden. Potatoes are one of the easiest vegetables for very small children to plant, and they delight in putting chunks of potatoes, just like the ones they see come home from the market, into the holes they have helped to dig. To make planting this garden easier for small children, use tomato transplants instead of seeds, and scatter plant the spinach.

A fall garden planted in late spring and early summer will yield not only summer vegetables, but also those for cool-weather soups. The pumpkins and potatoes can be stored to use as needed over the autumn months. If a container garden is preferred, all but the pumpkin plants can be included.

A planting of approximately six tomato plants, twenty-four bean plants, a bed of spinach, twelve potato plants, and six pumpkin plants will supply tomatoes, beans, and spinach for both summer and fall, while the potatoes, harvested in August or September, and September-harvest pumpkins will keep the fall soup pot full.

Prepare the garden site as directed on page 29. You will need a garden plot of about 120 square feet, divided into five eight-foot-long beds, four of them 1 foot wide and the fifth, for the pumpkins, 2 feet wide. Allow 1½-foot-wide walkways on one side of each bed. Plant the vegetables as directed in Chapter 3. The tomatoes, beans, and spinach will produce continuously over many weeks, but the potatoes and the pumpkins are a one-time harvest.

The pumpkin vines can become gigantic, so they should be pruned. As the vine grows, the first several flowers to appear will be male flowers. The first female flower will have a distinctive pumpkin-shaped base that will start to swell after the flower is pollinated. When this swelling begins, cut the vine just past the next leaf.

In addition to the recipes that follow, other soups can be made from the garden, including pumpkin, tomato, and mixed vegetable.

Sunflower Bean Poles

Sunflowers continue to grow and bloom throughout the summer months, so they work well doing double duty as supports for vining vegetables. Plant sunflower seeds, preferably those for a branching variety, in a single row, spacing them 2 feet apart. When the sunflower stalks are 2 to 3 feet high, plant vining beans, also called pole beans, in a circle around each stalk. The seeds should be spaced 6 inches apart and 6 inches from the stalk. As the beans grow, their vines will climb and twist around the sunflower stalk, using it for support and forming a tower of beans topped by a bright sunflower head.

Fall Garden Soup

At the end of summer, the garden is rich in ingredients for a full-bodied, one-pot meal, served with lots of crusty bread for dipping. This is a good dish to make with several children, as many hands will speed the preparation of the vegetables and add to the festive mood. Everyone can then sit down together to enjoy the soup they made themselves. Accompany the soup with baguettes or country-style bread.

$1/4$ cup olive oil

2 tablespoons unsalted butter

1 yellow or white onion, chopped

2 cloves garlic, minced

4 Yukon Gold, Red Rose, or other small, waxy
    boiling potatoes, cut into 1-inch cubes

2 cups trimmed, cut-up green beans

4 cups coarsely chopped spinach leaves

3 zucchini, cut into $1/2$-inch pieces

8 tomatoes, coarsely chopped

6 cups chicken, beef, or vegetable stock

2 tablespoons chopped fresh marjoram

1 tablespoon minced fresh thyme

Salt and freshly ground black pepper to taste

$1/4$ cup freshly grated Parmesan cheese
    (optional)

Put the olive oil and butter in a large soup pot over medium heat. When the butter is foaming, add the onion and garlic and sauté for 2 or 3 minutes, until the color changes. Add the potatoes and sauté for 2 or 3 minutes longer. Continue this process, adding the vegetables one at a time in the order given and then sautéing each one for 2 or 3 minutes before adding the next. Once the tomatoes have been added, pour in the stock. Bring to a boil over high heat, reduce the heat to low, cover, and cook, stirring occasionally, for $1^1/_2$ to 2 hours, or until all the vegetables are tender and the flavors have blended. The soup should be quite thick at this point. Add the marjoram and thyme, and season with salt and pepper. Ladle into bowls and serve piping hot, garnished with grated Parmesan, if desired.

SERVES 4 TO 6

Pumpkin and White Bean Soup
Served in a Pumpkin Tureen

Children love the surprise of taking the lid off a pumpkin to discover steaming soup inside. Transforming one pumpkin into a hot, nourishing soup and then using a second pumpkin as a serving bowl is a wonderful lesson in the origins of the food we eat. If you are in doubt about whether or not a particular pumpkin is good for cooking, choose a butternut squash instead, but still serve the soup in a pumpkin tureen. A French variety, 'Rouge d'Etampes,' or a 'Sugar Pie' baking pumpkin would be a good choice for cooking.

Small children can butter and season the pumpkin before it is baked, then once it is cool enough to handle, they can scrape out the soft meat. Older children can cook the beans and roast the peppers. Young children will enjoy pushing the button on the blender or food processor to purée the soup, and everyone will take pleasure in the final moment when the soup is ladled into its pumpkin tureen.

2 pumpkins, one about 10 pounds, the other
  about 8 pounds

2 tablespoons butter, cut into bits

1 cup dried Great Northern beans

6 cups water

2 teaspoons salt

1 bay leaf

3 or 4 sprigs of fresh thyme, each 4 inches long

2 red sweet peppers

$1^1/_2$ cups vegetable stock

1 teaspoon freshly ground black pepper

Preheat the oven to 350°. Cut the larger of the pumpkins into sections about 3 to 4 inches wide, scraping out and discarding the seeds and their fibers. Place the pumpkin slices on a baking sheet and dot them with the butter. Bake until very soft and tender, 2 to 2 1/2 hours. Remove and let stand until cool enough to handle. Scrape the soft meat from the skins; you should have 4 to 5 cups. Set aside. While the pumpkin is baking, rinse the beans and place in a pot with the water, 1 teaspoon of the salt, the bay leaf, and the thyme. Bring to a boil, reduce the heat to low, and simmer until the beans are tender and soft, about $1^1/_2$ hours. Drain, reserving the liquid. Cover the drained beans and set aside.

Preheat the broiler. Arrange the peppers on a baking sheet and broil until charred on all sides, about 3 to 5 minutes per side. Transfer to a plastic bag and let sweat for a few minutes, then peel away the skin. Slit each pepper in half and discard the stems, seeds, and ribs. Place peppers in a blender or food processor and add $^1/_2$ cup of the vegetable stock. Purée until smooth and transfer to a bowl.

Working in batches, if necessary, place the cooked pumpkin in the blender or food processor along with the remaining 1 cup vegetable stock and 1 cup of the reserved bean cooking liquid. Purée until smooth. Add the puréed peppers and process until combined. Pour into a soup pot and add the remaining 1 teaspoon of salt and the pepper. Place the pot over medium heat and stir often until the soup is hot, about 10 minutes. Stir in the reserved beans and cook for 5 minutes, or until the beans are heated thoroughly.

Meanwhile, to prepare the pumpkin tureen, slice off the upper one-quarter to one-third of the remaining pumpkin to make a lid. Using a metal spoon, scoop out all the seeds and any stringy bits from the interior and discard. Pour the hot soup into the tureen, place the lid on top, and bring to the table. To serve, remove the lid and ladle the hot soup into bowls.

SERVES 6 TO 8

Snap Bean and Potato Soup with Pasta

Mature snap beans that are beginning to develop peas inside the pods add a robust taste and texture to this dish. Younger children can snap the tails and stems from the beans, bending the stems back and pulling to remove any strings. Older children can cut the potatoes and do the initial sautéing.

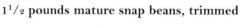

2 slices bacon, coarsely chopped

2 tablespoons olive oil

2 cloves garlic, minced

$^1/_2$ yellow onion, minced

$1^1/_2$ pounds mature snap beans, trimmed

6 cups water

1 tablespoon chopped fresh thyme

$^1/_2$ pound small, waxy boiling potatoes,
      cut into 1-inch pieces

$^1/_4$ cup broken spaghetti or other pasta

Salt to taste

1 teaspoon freshly ground black pepper

$^1/_4$ cup freshly grated Parmesan cheese

In a heavy saucepan, heat the bacon in the olive oil over medium heat until it begins to render its fat. Add the garlic and onion, and sauté for 2 to 3 minutes. Add the beans and cook, stirring, for 2 to 3 minutes. Add the water and thyme and bring to a boil. Reduce the heat to low, cover, and cook for about 30 minutes, or until the beans are tender. Add the potatoes and cook for another 20 minutes, or until the potatoes are tender and the beans can easily be cut with a fork. Using a wooden spoon or a fork, mash some of the potatoes to thicken the soup. Add the pasta and cook for 10 minutes longer, or until the pasta is done. Season with the salt and pepper and ladle the soup into bowls. Pass the Parmesan cheese at the table.

SERVES 4 TO 6

A Winter Pantry Garden
Tomatoes, Sunflowers, Shelling Beans, and Strawberries

The summer garden can be filled with plants whose bounty can be preserved and enjoyed during the winter months. Sunflower seeds make healthful snacks or wonderfully crunchy ingredients in breads and salads. Dried beans can be used in soups and stews, while home-made dried tomatoes will make all manner of dishes, from soups and stews to pastas, sparkle. Strawberry jam can be spread atop pancakes or toast, or used as a filling for cakes and cookies.

The tasks associated with drying and preserving these simple foods are easy ones that can be performed by children of all ages. Even making the strawberry jam requires almost no cooking, and it is a revelatory experience for children to cook from a pantry they helped to stock.

A planting of approximately six tomato plants, twelve strawberry plants, twelve bean plants, and one row of sunflowers will supply a well-stocked winter pantry. The garden plot will need to measure about 75 square feet, or everything can be planted in containers if dwarf sunflower varieties are chosen. Garden activities are all easy ones for young children to participate in. Large-seeded sunflowers and beans are simple to sow, while the strawberries are grown from transplants. For ease of planting, tomato transplants are the best choice.

Plan on six beds, each 1 foot wide and 10 to 12 feet long, with a $1^{1}/_{2}$-foot-wide path on one side of each bed. Plant the sunflowers where they won't shade out the smaller plants as they grow.

The tomatoes can be harvested and dried whenever they are ripe (see page 112). Strawberries can be picked and made into jam (see page 107) the moment they are red, sweet, and ripe, usually late spring through summer. The sunflower seeds and the beans are harvested once the plants have dried down, usually late summer or fall. (see Gathering Sunflower Seeds, page 30, and Drying Beans, page 35.)

Easy Strawberry Jam

This recipe for freezer jam requires only 1 minute of cooking, which can be supervised by an adult. Crushing the berries, stirring them with sugar, and pouring the jam into jars are all activities in which small children can participate. The jam is never as thick as traditional cooked jam, but the texture is just right for spooning on toast or over ice cream. (Note: Do not increase recipe, as jam may not set in larger quantities.)

1 quart ripe strawberries, at room temperature

4 cups sugar

1 box (1.75 ounces) Sure-Jell® fruit pectin

³/₄ cup water

Remove the stems from the strawberries. Wash them and put them into a colander to drain. Once drained, place them in a bowl and crush them with a potato masher. They should be in coarse pieces, but not puréed. Measure 2 cups, and reserve any extra for another use. Put the 2 cups of strawberries in a bowl with exactly 4 cups of sugar. Stir thoroughly. Set aside for 10 minutes, stirring occasionally.

In a small saucepan, combine the water and the pectin. Over high heat, bring the mixture to a boil, stirring constantly. Boil for only 1 minute, then remove from the heat. Stir the hot pectin mixture into the strawberry/sugar mixture and stir constantly for about 3 minutes until the sugar is completely dissolved and no crystals are apparent. Let stand at room temperature for 24 hours.

If you are going to freeze the jam, pour it into plastic freezer-proof containers with fitted lids. It will keep for up to one year in the freezer. If you are going to refrigerate the jam, you may use glass canning jars with wire bale lids and fitted rubber rings, or canning jars with screw-top rings and fitted lids. The jam will keep for up to 3 weeks in the refrigerator.

MAKES ABOUT 2 PINTS

Pasta Salad with Dried Tomatoes

Dried tomatoes packed in oil are used here, as the flavorsome oil is incorporated into the salad dressing. Other sturdy pastas—rigatoni, penne, fusilli —can substitute for the tortellini, and other vegetables can be added as well. Children can cut the tomatoes with blunt scissors and mix together the salad ingredients in the bowl. Because of the boiling water, however, only adults should cook the pasta.

8 quarts water

1 teaspoon salt

10 ounces tortellini

8 oil-packed dried tomatoes, drained and minced

1 clove garlic, minced

$1/4$ cup olive oil from the tomatoes

$1/4$ cup olive oil

$1/4$ cup chopped black olives

$1/2$ cup minced red onion

1 teaspoon fresh thyme leaves

$1/2$ teaspoon freshly ground black pepper

1 cup crumbled feta cheese

Bring the water to a boil in a large pot. Add the salt and the pasta, and cook until al dente (tender, but firm to the bite). Drain the pasta and place in a bowl. Add the tomatoes, garlic, the oil from the tomatoes, the olive oil, olives, onion, thyme, and pepper. Let cool to room temperature, or let cool to room temperature, cover, and refrigerate until slightly chilled.

When ready to serve, add all but 2 tablespoons of the feta cheese. Turn to mix the ingredients well. Transfer the salad to a serving bowl and garnish with the remaining cheese.

SERVES 4 TO 6

CHAPTER SIX

Kitchen Notes

Cooking with children is one of the most entertaining—and often messy—activities that parents and teachers can engage in, yet it is also one of the most rewarding. The more children can do on their own—actually do, not simply watch being done—the more meaningful and exciting their experiences will be. Cooking, especially cooking from the garden, is more than developing skill in following instructions and in perfecting techniques. It is a creative, inventive experience that relies on intuition and experimentation to develop an innate sense and feel for the way good food tastes and looks.

The kitchen, like the garden, must be a safe place for children to work and to play. There should be adult supervision in the kitchen when boiling water, stove tops, ovens, knives, and machines of any kind are being used. On the other hand, stirring one ingredient into another, such as chives into cream cheese, can be done without danger by even the smallest child. Making a salad of torn lettuce leaves and turning them with a vinaigrette, arranging fresh vegetables on a platter, spreading bread with herbed butter, and shelling peas or beans are all tasks small children can accomplish on their own.

Before the actual preparation of a recipe begins, a child must be taught how important it is to wash and dry his or her hands before handling any equipment or food. The next step is to assemble the necessary tools—a whisk, measuring cup and spoons, saucepan,

Drying Tomatoes

Sun-drying tomatoes is a project for children who live in areas with hot, dry summers. Damp climates, whether coastal or inland, have too much humidity for successful drying. In those regions, tomatoes can be dried in the oven.

Oven-Drying

Preheat an oven to 200°. Slice the tomatoes as for sun-drying, and place the slices in single layers on baking sheets. Bake, turning the slices over every hour, for 2 to 3 hours, until the tomatoes are dry but not brittle. Store as directed for sundried tomatoes, opposite page.

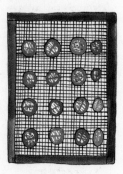

wooden spoon—and the ingredients, and to learn about the role of each during the process. This is how children become familiar with the kitchen, its tools, and its pantry.

In sum, we should know that the infant's sense of taste is developed very early (beginning in the womb) and that it goes through different stages which are more or less irreversible. It is best not to rush these stages. Each child's individual taste should be respected.

—From *Le Goût et L'Enfant* (*Taste and the Child*)
by Jacques Puisais

Experimentation should be encouraged. If a child suggests using basil instead of tarragon, or green beans instead of corn in a recipe, and is allowed to make the substitution, the sense of achievement and pride in the completed dish will soar.

If flour spills, milk splashes, and eggs tumble, if clothes are splattered with tomato sauce, or the floor is sticky with orange juice, think of the kitchen as a laboratory for learning, one that can be cleaned and made pristine for the next experiment. Cleaning the laboratory is part of the process, a part that children should participate in to complete their sense of pride.

Summer Salsa

All of the vegetables in this mild salsa are ready to harvest at the same time. To make the preparation of the recipe more child friendly, do the chopping in a food processor rather than with a sharp knife. Serve the salsa with chips or sliced vegetables. To change the flavor of the salsa, add a little mango or cantaloupe.

To make a drying rack, take an old window-screen frame and fit it with fine stainless steel or plastic mesh. A staple gun or electrical tape can be used to secure the edges. Select a spot that receives full sun and place the drying rack atop sawhorses or any other base that allows for good air circulation.

3 large tomatoes, seeded and coarsely chopped

1 small fresh jalapeño chile, seeded and minced

1 clove garlic, minced

2 tablespoons finely chopped cilantro

2 tomatillos, husks removed and finely chopped

Juice from 1 small lime

$^1/_4$ teaspoon salt

$^1/_4$ teaspoon freshly ground black pepper

Cut ripe tomatoes crosswise into 1/4-inch-thick slices and place them on the screen about 1 inch apart. Leave the tomatoes to dry for 3 to 5 days, bringing them inside to a sheltered location at night to protect them from the evening dew. They are ready when they have a supple and leathery texture. They should be neither tacky nor brittle. Once dried, store them in airtight tins, lock-top plastic bags, or immersed in olive oil in jars.

In a small bowl, combine the tomatoes, chile, garlic, cilantro, tomatillos, lime juice, salt, and pepper. Stir together until well blended. Cover and chill for at least 30 minutes or for up to 1 hour before serving. Keeps for up to 4 days in the refrigerator.

MAKES ABOUT 2 CUPS

Steamed Baby Artichokes

Baby artichokes are tender enough to eat whole and can be cooked without any trimming. If they are very young, the stems can be eaten as well. This recipe is easy to prepare, although adult supervision is necessary because of the need for boiling water. Herb mayonnaise (page 85) or vinaigrette is perfect for dipping these tender, steamed buds.

About 8 cups water (enough to fill the bottom of a large steamer)

12 baby artichokes

Bring the water to a boil in the bottom of a large steamer. Place the artichokes on the steamer rack, cover the steamer, and cook about 20 minutes, or until easily pierced all the way through with a knife. Remove from the steamer and rinse with cold water to halt the cooking process.

Serve at room temperature or cold.

SERVES 4

Mesclun Salad

Salads are simple ventures that children can do on their own. Encourage them to experiment with different herbs for the dressing. Mesclun is a mixture of different loose-leaf lettuces, such as green and red oak leaf, Lolla Rosa, and Tango varieties, plus other greens such as chicory, radicchio, escarole, and herbs including arugula and chives. In Provence, mesclun *means "mixture," and some classic mixtures include as many as twenty-one different ingredients. Premixed packages of seeds can be purchased to plant in your personal salad garden.*

¹/₃ pound mixed baby salad greens

DRESSING

    1 teaspoon Dijon mustard

    1 teaspoon red wine vinegar

    1 small clove garlic, minced

    Pinch of salt

    ¹/₄ teaspoon freshly ground black pepper

    ¹/₄ cup extra virgin olive oil

Carefully wash and dry the greens and place them in a large bowl. To make the dressing, combine the mustard, vinegar, garlic, salt, and pepper in a small bowl and mix together with a fork or small whisk. Slowly drizzle the olive oil into the mustard mixture, stirring constantly. This will create a thick, creamy emulsion.

Drizzle the dressing over the greens. Toss well and serve immediately.

SERVES 4

Heart of Romaine Salad with Creamy Feta Dressing

Anyone who likes thick, creamy dressings and garlicky croutons will love this salad. You can also use old-fashioned iceberg lettuce instead of romaine. Children will enjoy making the croutons and the dressing.

CROUTONS

2 to 3 cups cubed (1-inch cubes) day-old baguette
or similar bread

2 cloves garlic

2 tablespoons olive oil

DRESSING

3 to 4 ounces feta cheese

1/3 cup half-and-half

1/4 teaspoon salt

1/4 teaspoon freshly ground black pepper

1 teaspoon finely grated lemon zest

GREENS

1 head romaine lettuce

To make the croutons, preheat the oven to 400°. Rub the bread cubes on all sides with the garlic cloves. Evenly coat the bottom of a baking sheet with the olive oil and roll the croutons in the olive oil until well coated. Bake in the oven, turning occasionally, for 15 to 20 minutes, or until golden brown. Remove from the oven and set aside.

To prepare the dressing, crumble the feta cheese into a small bowl and mash with a fork until it is in pea-sized pieces. Slowly drizzle in the half-and-half, stirring constantly. Add the salt, pepper, and lemon zest. Cover and refrigerate for up to 30 minutes.

Remove the darker green outer leaves of the lettuce head; discard the damaged ones and reserve any good ones for another use. Cut off the stem ends from the pale, yellow green inner leaves. Arrange the leaves on a large plate or shallow bowl. Pour the dressing evenly over the greens and top with the croutons. Serve at once.

SERVES 4

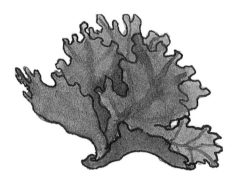

French Green Bean Salad

With the supervision of adults, children can trim the stems from the green beans and cook them, create the vinaigrette, and toss the salad together.

2 quarts water

1 teaspoon salt

$^3/_4$ pound French-style green beans, stem end removed

1 teaspoon olive oil

$^1/_2$ cup finely chopped walnuts

VINAIGRETTE

1$^1/_2$ tablespoons olive oil

1 teaspoon fresh lemon juice

Salt and pepper to taste

1 tablespoon minced fresh dill

Bring the water to a full boil and add the salt and the green beans. Cook until just barely tender, about 5 minutes. Pour the green beans into a strainer and run cold water over them to halt the cooking process.

To prepare the walnuts, heat the teaspoon of olive oil in a small skillet over medium heat. Add the walnuts and turn in the olive oil to coat completely. Toast until they begin to turn golden brown, about 3 to 4 minutes. Remove from the heat and set aside.

To prepare the vinaigrette, in a medium-size mixing bowl, stir together the olive oil, lemon juice, salt, pepper, and dill. Add the green beans and toss to coat well with the vinaigrette. Transfer the salad to a serving dish and top with the toasted walnuts.

SERVES 4

Roasted Potato Salad

This is a flavorful potato salad that makes a nice change from traditional mayonnaise-based salads. Children will have fun preparing the ingredients and assembling the salad.

1 tablespoon olive oil

1 teaspoon salt

1 teaspoon freshly ground black pepper

2 pounds red potatoes, cut into 1-inch cubes

6 whole cloves garlic, peeled

VINAIGRETTE

$^1/_3$ cup finely chopped Italian parsley

2 cloves garlic, minced

2 tablespoons olive oil

1 teaspoon red wine vinegar

$^1/_4$ teaspoon salt

$^1/_4$ teaspoon freshly ground black pepper

Preheat the oven to 450°. In a large bowl, combine the olive oil, salt, and pepper. Mix well and toss the potatoes and garlic cloves in the mixture until well coated. Spread the potatoes out on a baking sheet, creating one layer. Bake, turning often, until the potatoes can be easily pierced with the tines of a fork and are crisp and golden brown, about 45 minutes. Remove the potatoes from the oven and set aside.

To prepare the vinaigrette, combine the parsley, garlic, olive oil, vinegar, salt, and pepper in a medium salad bowl. Add the potatoes and toss until well coated. Serve immediately.

SERVES 4

Basic Vegetable Stock

This is a very simple vegetable stock that children can prepare with adult supervision. The vegetables are just tossed into a soup pot and allowed to boil for up to an hour until they release all their flavor to make a rich, savory broth.

10 cups water

4 celery stalks, cut into 2-inch pieces

4 medium carrots, cut into 2-inch pieces

1 onion, quartered

2 cups button mushrooms, halved or quartered

6 cloves garlic, peeled

2 teaspoons salt

1 teaspoon freshly ground black pepper

2 fresh or dried bay leaves

Bring the water to a full boil and add all the remaining ingredients. Allow the stock to boil uncovered for 45 minutes to 1 hour. Pour through a colander to strain out the vegetables, which will have released all their flavor into the stock. Use immediately or refrigerate for up to 4 days. The stock can also be frozen for up to 6 months.

MAKES 6 CUPS

Cold Cucumber Soup

This chilled, pale green summer soup is easy for children to prepare and has a delicate flavor they will enjoy.

2 tablespoons butter

2 cucumbers, peeled and cut into 1-inch pieces

1 leek (white part only) cut into 1/2-inch slices

1 fresh bay leaf

1 tablespoon flour

3 cups Basic Vegetable Stock (see page 120)

$^1/_2$ teaspoon salt

$^1/_2$ cup cream

Zest of 1 lemon

1 tablespoon freshly squeezed lemon juice

1 teaspoon finely chopped fresh dill

$^1/_2$ teaspoon freshly ground black pepper

$^1/_4$ cup sour cream

Melt the butter in a saucepan over medium heat. When it begins to foam, add the cucumber, leek, and bay leaf and sauté until tender, about 20 minutes. Reduce the heat to low if the vegetables begin to brown.

Stir in the flour, then add the vegetable stock and salt. Cover and simmer for 30 minutes. Remove from the heat and allow to cool to room temperature. Remove the bay leaf, then blend the soup with an electric mixer or food processor. Stir in the cream, lemon zest, lemon juice, dill, and pepper. Chill for at least 30 minutes and up to 1 hour. Serve with a dollop of sour cream.

SERVES 4

Parsley and Potato Soup

This flavorful, creamy soup has a mild spiciness that makes it a nice introduction to spices for young children.

3 tablespoons olive oil

2 yellow onions, chopped

2 cloves garlic, minced

1 dried pasilla chile pepper, ground (about
    1 tablespoon)

3 cups Basic Vegetable Stock (see page 120)

4 cups water

6 large potatoes, peeled, quartered, and boiled
    until tender

1 teaspoon salt

1 teaspoon freshly ground black pepper

4 cups coarsely chopped Italian parsley leaves,
    about 1 bunch

1 lemon (for garnish)

Heat the olive oil in a large pot. Add the onions, garlic, and chile pepper. Cook over medium heat until onions are translucent, about 15 minutes. Add half the stock and bring to a boil. Let boil for 5 minutes, then reduce the heat, cover, and simmer for 15 minutes. Add the remaining stock and the water. Bring to a boil again, reduce the heat, and let simmer another 10 minutes. Add the potatoes, salt, and pepper and continue cooking for 5 more minutes. Remove from the heat and stir in the parsley. Purée the soup in batches in a food processor or blender. Serve hot, garnished with slices of lemon.

SERVES 8

Fresh Pea Soup

Children can have fun shelling the fresh peas and pushing the blender button to purée this very simple soup. Serve the soup hot or cold, with a decorative swirl of sour cream if desired.

4 cups chicken or vegetable stock

3 cups shelled fresh peas (about 2 pounds unshelled)

1 clove garlic

1 teaspoon grated ginger

$^1/_4$ teaspoon salt (optional)

1 sprig mint

Sour cream (optional)

Bring the stock to a gentle boil in a soup pot. Add the peas, garlic, and ginger, reduce the heat, and simmer for about 20 minutes, or until the peas are soft. Remove from the heat and let cool to room temperature. Purée the cooled soup in a blender or food processor or with a hand mixer. Pour into a clean saucepan and reheat to serving temperature. Taste and add the salt, if needed. (If the stock was well seasoned, you may not need the salt.) Ladle into bowls and top each serving with 1 or 2 mint leaves. Serve immediately. Alternatively, cover and chill the puréed soup, adjusting with salt just before serving. Garnish soup with a swirl of sour cream, if desired.

SERVES 4

Roasted Butternut Squash Soup

This thick, creamy soup has a rich nutty flavor, lightly seasoned with thyme. Enlist young children to help sauté the aromatics and squash and to purée the soup.

2 butternut squashes, about 2 pounds total weight

4 cups vegetable stock

1 teaspoon unsalted butter

1 teaspoon olive oil

1 small yellow onion, minced

1 clove garlic, minced

1 teaspoon minced fresh thyme

¹/₄ teaspoon salt (optional)

¹/₄ cup freshly grated Parmesan cheese

¹/₂ teaspoon freshly ground black pepper

Preheat the oven to 450°. Halve the squashes lengthwise and scoop out and discard the seeds. Cut the squash halves into 3-inch squares. Place the pieces, skin side down, on a baking sheet. Bake about 35 to 40 minutes, until the pieces can be easily pierced with the tines of a fork. Remove from the oven and, when cool enough to handle, scrape the pulp from the skins. Set aside.

Pour the stock into a heavy saucepan and place over high heat. Bring to a gentle boil. Melt the butter with the olive oil in a large skillet over medium heat. Add the onion, garlic, and thyme and sauté until translucent, about 5 minutes. Add the squash pulp and sauté for 2 to 3 minutes. Add the squash mixture to the stock and cook over medium heat for 30 minutes. Remove from the heat and let cool.

Purée the soup, pour into a clean saucepan, and reheat. Add the salt, if needed. Ladle into bowls and sprinkle with cheese and pepper.

SERVES 6

Herbed Cream Cheese Sandwiches

Cream cheese sandwiches are perfect for a small tea party or summer pic-nic. They are simple to prepare and can easily be modified to include dif-ferent vegetables.

4 tomatoes

1 yellow bell pepper

1 red bell pepper

1 cup **Cream Cheese with Chives** (see page 83)

1 loaf thinly sliced sourdough bread

$^1/_4$ pound baby lettuce greens

1 cucumber, peeled and thinly sliced

Slice the tomatoes and bell peppers into very thin slices. Spread an even amount of cream cheese on each slice of bread, using about 1 tablespoon per sandwich. Then add a leaf or two of baby greens and slices of cucumber, tomato, and peppers. Cut the sandwiches in half diagonally. Serve immediately.

MAKES ABOUT 16 SANDWICHES

Roasted Vegetable Sandwiches

These garden-fresh sandwiches are delicious and easy to make. To vary the recipe, try using roasted eggplant instead of, or in addition to, the zucchini, or replace the fresh tomatoes with sun-dried ones (see page 113).

2 zucchini, sliced lengthwise into
  $^1/_2$-inch-thick slices

Olive oil and salt for roasting

1 baguette or 2 panini or other long rolls

$^1/_2$ teaspoon minced garlic

$^1/_2$ teaspoon salt

Freshly ground pepper

6 ounces mozzarella or jack cheese, thinly sliced

1 large tomato, thinly sliced

Handful of fresh basil leaves, thinly sliced

Preheat the oven to 450°. Arrange the zucchini slices in a single layer on a baking sheet and brush lightly with olive oil. Season with salt and roast until golden, about 5 minutes per side.

Preheat the broiler. Split the baguette or rolls in half lengthwise. Place, cut side up, on a baking sheet. In a small bowl, whisk together the olive oil, garlic, salt, and pepper. Brush the tops of the bread with the oil mixture and broil until crisp, less than 1 minute.

Remove the bread from the broiler and top half the slices with cheese and half with zucchini. Return the cheese-covered halves to the broiler just until the cheese melts. Top the zucchini with a layer of tomato slices, brush lightly with olive oil, and sprinkle with basil. Cover with the melted cheese halves, slice, and serve.

MAKES 4 SANDWICHES

Puff Pastry-Topped Ratatouille

With supervision, children can personalize these individual ratatouilles by cutting their initials, instead of standard vents, in the top of the puff pastry. If you don't have the fresh herbs growing in your kitchen garden, substitute 1 teaspoon dried herbs de provence.

4 teaspoons extra virgin olive oil

2 cloves garlic, minced

4 tomatoes, cut into medium dice

1 teaspoon finely minced fresh marjoram leaves

1 teaspoon finely minced fresh thyme leaves

Freshly ground black pepper to taste

Pinch of salt

1 red bell pepper, cut into medium dice

2 small zucchini, cut into medium dice

2 small yellow squash, cut into medium dice

2 ears corn, kernels cut off the cob

1 sheet thawed frozen puff pastry (about 9 ounces)

Preheat the oven to 425°.

In a small sauté pan, heat 2 teaspoons of the olive oil over medium-high heat. Add the garlic and saute until translucent. Add the tomatoes, herbs, pepper, and salt. Lower the heat to medium and cook, stirring occasionally, for 10 minutes.

Meanwhile, in a medium saucepan, heat the remaining 2 teaspoons of olive oil over medium-high heat. Add the bell pepper and sauté for 4 minutes. Add the zucchini and squash and sauté for another 4 minutes. Add the corn and cook just until the kernels are heated through. Add the tomato mixture, and remove from the heat. Divide the vegetable mixture equally among four 1-cup ramekins.

Gently unfold the puff pastry sheet on a lightly floured work surface. With a lightly floured rolling pin, roll out the puff pastry to $^1/_8$ inch thick. Using one of the ramekins as a guide, cut four 5-inch circles out of the puff pastry. Place one of the circles on top of a vegetable-filled ramekin and crimp the edge against the rim of the ramekin to seal. Repeat with the remaining 3 ramekins. With the tip of a sharp knife, carefully cut a vent in the puff pastry. Place the ramekins on a baking sheet and bake for 15 minutes. Let cool on a rack for 10 minutes, then serve.

SERVES 4

Vegetable Pockets

These pastry pockets are fun to make and to eat. If desired, the puff pastry can be cut into even smaller squares to make bite-size treats to serve as appetizers. The filling can also be modifed to include a child's favorite vegetables.

$^3/_4$ **cup vegetable broth**

1 shallot, minced

1 medium carrot, julienned

1 bunch leeks, white part only

2 small zucchini, sliced

1 bunch chard (about 4 loosely packed cups)

$^1/_4$ **teaspoon freshly ground pepper**

$^1/_4$ **teaspoon celery seed**

$^1/_4$ **cup chopped parsley**

1 cup grated Swiss cheese

1 sheet thawed frozen puff pastry (about 9 ounces)

Heat $^1/_2$ cup of the broth in a large skillet. Add the shallot and cook for 5 minutes over medium heat. Add the carrot and leeks and cook 3 minutes, then add the chard, zucchini, and the remaining broth and cook for 3 minutes more. Remove from heat and drain well through a sieve. Add pepper, celery seed, parsley, and cheese. Taste and adjust seasoning.

Preheat the oven to 400°. Gently unfold the puff pastry sheet on a lightly floured work surface. Cut the pastry into 9 squares. Roll each square out to approximately 5 x 6 inches. Place about $^1/_3$ cup of the vegetable mixture in the center of the square and fold the corners in, pinching or twisting to seal. Place on a baking sheet and bake for 15 minutes, or until the pastry is crisp and lightly browned. Let cool slightly before serving.

SERVES 3 OR 4

Spinach and Artichoke Cake

This dish, which is basically a thick omelette, can be varied endlessly with the addition of different vegetables and herbs. Escarole and sorrel make delicious substitutions for the spinach, and grated Parmesan can be added for extra flavor.

4 medium artichokes

2 tablespoons olive oil

1 yellow onion, diced

$^1/_2$ pound spinach leaves, well washed

6 eggs

$^1/_2$ cup whole milk

Finely chopped parsley and thyme to taste

Salt, pepper, and nutmeg to taste

1 tablespoon sweet butter

Trim the artichokes. Slice the hearts and cook them in boiling water for 6 to 8 minutes, then set aside. Heat half the oil, then add the onions and cook gently for 3 to 4 minutes. Add the spinach and cook for another 2 minutes.

Beat the eggs, milk, chopped herbs, and spices together. Combine the egg mixture with the vegetables. In a nonstick sauté pan, melt the butter with the remaining oil, add the egg-vegetable mixture, and cook for 3 to 4 minutes on medium heat. Next, bake at 375° for 10 minutes, or until lightly browned. Let cool for a few minutes and turn the cake onto a platter. Serve warm or at room temperature.

SERVES 3 TO 4

Garden Gratin

Children who are comfortable using knives and working at the stove can make this simple dish on their own with adult supervision. If children are new to the kitchen, put them in charge of grating the cheese and bread crumbs with a handheld grater and assembling the dish before baking.

3 tablespoons olive oil

1 small yellow onion, finely chopped

1 tablespoon minced fresh thyme

1 globe eggplant, sliced into $1/4$-inch-thick
    rounds

3 small zucchini or other summer squashes,
    sliced into $1/4$-inch-thick rounds

$1/4$ teaspoon salt

$1/2$ teaspoon freshly ground black pepper

3 tomatoes, sliced crosswise into $1/4$-inch-thick
    rounds

1 cup grated Gruyère cheese

$1/2$ cup freshly grated Parmesan cheese

$1/4$ cup fine dried bread crumbs

Preheat the oven to 400°. Heat 2 tablespoons of the olive oil in a large skillet over medium heat. Add the onion and thyme and sauté until the onion begins to turn translucent, about 3 minutes. Add the eggplant, zucchini, salt, and pepper and turn them in the pan two or three times to coat them with the oil. Reduce the heat to low, cover, and cook until the eggplant and zucchini are tender and can easily be pierced with the tines of a fork, about 10 minutes. Remove from the heat.

To assemble the gratin, layer about one-quarter of the eggplant mixture in an ungreased, shallow 8 x 8-inch baking dish. Top with a layer of tomatoes and then one-quarter of the Gruyère and Parmesan cheeses. Repeat the layering process until you have used up the vegetables, creating three to four layers. Cover the top with the remaining cheese and the bread crumbs, and drizzle with the remaining tablespoon of olive oil.

Bake for 30 to 40 minutes, or until tender all the way through when pierced with a knife. The juices should be bubbling at the sides. Serve immediately directly from the dish.

SERVES 4

Oven Fries

Other root or tuber vegetables, such as sweet potatoes, taro root, and Jerusalem artichokes, can be used in this dish. Children who are comfortable using knives can make this on their own with adult supervision. Serve as a main dish with salad greens or as a side dish to accompany grilled pork chops or spicy sausages. Serve with herb mayonnaise (page 85).

3 large potatoes

3 carrots

4 parsnips

2 tablespoons light vegetable oil

1/4 teaspoon salt

1/2 teaspoon freshly ground black pepper

Preheat the oven to 450°. Cut the potatoes, carrots, and parsnips into strips 2 inches long, ¹/₂ inch wide, and ¹/₂ inch thick. Place in a large bowl and add the oil, salt, and pepper. Toss to coat lightly. Transfer the vegetables to a baking sheet, arranging them in a single layer. Bake for 40 to 45 minutes, or until tender on the inside when pierced with a fork and nicely crisp on the outside. Serve immediately.

SERVES 6 TO 8

French Crepes with Fresh Fruit

Crepes are easy for children to make, although adult supervision is necessary. With the right type of small, nonstick skillet, children can even practice flipping the crepes in the pan, a skill that is sure to impress their young friends. The crepes can be made up to a day in advance, stored stacked in the refrigerator, and filled just before serving. Chopped peaches, sliced bananas, kiwifruit, or whole blackberries can be substituted for the strawberries.

CREPES

    1 cup all-purpose flour

    1 cup milk

    2 eggs, lightly beaten

    $1/4$ teaspoon salt

    1 teaspoon pure vanilla extract

    Unsalted butter

FILLING

    2 cups fresh strawberries, hulled and coarsely chopped

    2 tablespoons confectioners' sugar

To make the crepes, place the flour in a bowl and slowly whisk in the milk. Make sure to go slowly, as this helps to prevent lumps from forming. Whisk in the eggs, salt, and vanilla. The batter should be the consistency of heavy cream. Set aside to sit for at least 15 minutes, or for up to 30 minutes. This gives time for the air bubbles to pop, which will result in beautifully flat pancakes.

To cook the crepes, melt about $1/4$ teaspoon butter over medium heat in a 6-inch nonstick skillet. When the butter begins to foam, swirl the skillet to coat the entire bottom. Lift the skillet from the heat and pour just under $1/4$ cup batter into the center of it. Again swirl it gently so that the batter coats the bottom evenly. Return the skillet to the heat and cook for 1 to 2 minutes, until the crepe is opaque and no longer liquid. Turn the crepe over and cook for another 30 seconds, then transfer it to a plate. Repeat with the remaining batter, adding another $1/4$ teaspoon butter to the pan after cooking every 2 or 3 crepes.

To assemble the crepes, place about 3 tablespoons of the strawberries down the center of each crepe. Fold in the edges from either side to the center so that they overlap. Transfer to a serving plate, seam side down, and lightly dust the tops with the confectioners' sugar.

MAKES 10 TO 12 CREPES, EACH ABOUT 6 INCHES IN DIAMETER.

Cherry Clafouti

Traditionally made during cherry season in France, this classic dessert can also be made with other fruits, such as halved figs, plums, apricots, and quartered peaches. Children can help pit the cherries and whisk together the batter, and it is fun for them to see the clafouti rise to nearly three times its original height in the oven before collapsing the moment it begins to cool.

BATTER

> 3 eggs, lightly beaten
>
> 1¹/₄ cups milk
>
> 1 cup flour
>
> 1 teaspoon pure vanilla extract, or 1 vanilla bean

FILLING

> 1 cup cherries, pitted
>
> 1 teaspoon unsalted butter

Preheat the oven to 375°. Grease the bottom and sides of a 9-inch square baking dish that is at least 2 inches deep.

To make the batter, whisk together the eggs and milk in a bowl until blended. Slowly whisk in the flour; do not hurry this step or lumps may form. Mix in the vanilla extract, or split the vanilla bean lengthwise and, using the tip of a knife, scrape the seeds into the batter.

Cover the bottom of the baking dish with the cherries. Pour the batter over the cherries, being careful not to dislodge them. Dot the batter with the butter. Bake for 35 to 40 minutes, or until the batter has nearly tripled in size, the top is golden brown, and a knife inserted into the center comes out clean. Remove from the oven and serve warm or at room temperature.

SERVES 6 TO 8

Zucchini Bread

This perennial favorite makes good use of an overabundant supply of zucchini. Even young children can help prepare the batter, but an adult should grate the squash.

2 cups flour

$^3/_4$ teaspoon cinnamon

$^1/_2$ teaspoon salt

$^3/_4$ teaspoon baking soda

$^3/_4$ teaspoon baking powder

2/3 cup vegetable oil

$1^1/_3$ cups sugar

2 eggs

$^1/_2$ teaspoon pure vanilla extract

2 cups grated zucchini (about 3 zucchini)

$^1/_3$ cup chopped walnuts

Preheat oven to 325°. Rub one 9 x 5-inch loaf pan with soft butter. Add a small handful of flour to the pan and tilt the pan to coat evenly; shake out extra flour.

Over a mixing bowl, sift together the flour, cinnamon, salt, baking soda, and baking powder. In a separate mixing bowl, beat together the oil, sugar, eggs, and vanilla until smooth and creamy. Add the sifted ingredients to the egg mixture and stir to combine well. Stir in the zucchini and walnuts. Pour the batter into the prepared pan and bake for 1 hour, or until a toothpick comes out clean when inserted in the middle of the loaf. Invert the pan to remove the loaf, then place the bread on rack to cool.

MAKES 1 LOAF

Resources

Vegetable Seeds

Johnny's Selected Seeds
310 Foss Hill Road
Albion, ME 04910
(207) 437-9294

This company offers a wide selection of vegetable seeds, with a particular focus on short-season vegetables. Free catalog.

Pinetree Garden Seeds
P.O. Box 300
New Gloucester, ME 04260
(207) 926-3400

Many unusual vegetable seeds are available, including 45 different tomato varieties. Free catalog.

Seeds of Change
P.O. Box 15700
Santa Fe, NM 87506
(888) 762-7333

Certified organic, open-pollinated vegetable seeds grown by family farms. Many heirloom, traditional, and unique varieties, plus seed potatoes and garlic, herbs, and cover crops. Free catalog.

Shepherd's Garden Seeds
616 Highway 9
Felton, CA 95018
(408) 335-6910
(408) 335-2080 Fax

The catalog lists a number of European specialty vegetables, including recent hybrids and heirlooms. Flower seeds are also available. Illustrated with single-color artwork. Catalog costs $1.00.

Flower Seeds

Seeds of Change
P.O. Box 15700
Santa Fe, NM 87506
(888) 762-7333

A wonderful collection of flowers, including many varieties of sunflowers; all organically grown and open-pollinated. Free color catalog.

Shepherd's Garden Seeds
616 Highway 9
Felton, CA 95018
(408) 335-6910
(408) 335-2080 Fax

A number of interesting flower varieties, as well as collections of flower seeds, are offered along with vegetable seeds. Catalog costs $1.00.

Thompson & Morgan
P.O. Box 1308
Jackson, NJ 08527-0308
(908) 363-2225
(908) 363-9356 Fax

Although the catalog includes vegetable as well as flower seeds, the flower seeds, many of them unusual, take up 80 percent of the more than 200 pages of listings. Illustrated with full-color photographs. Free catalog.

All-Purpose Suppliers

Park Seed Company
Cokesbury Road
Greenwood, SC 29647
(803) 223-7333
(803) 941-4206 Fax

An interesting selection of vegetable, herb, and flower seeds; bulbs; perennial plants; and herb plants are offered. Free catalog.

W. Atlee Burpee & Co.
P.O. Box 5114
Warminster, PA 18974
(215) 674-9633

This well-known company offers a standard selection of vegetable and flower seeds and perennial plants. Free catalog.

Harmony Farm Supply
Warehouse Store
3244 Gravenstein Highway North
Sebastopol, CA 95472
P.O. Box 460
Graton, CA 95444
(707) 823-9125
(707) 823-1734

This company has a wide selection of organic products of all kinds, plus bare-root fruit trees in season and books. Catalog costs $2.00.

The Natural Gardening Company
217 San Anselmo Avenue
San Anselmo, CA 94960
(707) 766-9303
(707) 766-9747 Fax

This company has a fine selection of organic garden products, including fertilizers and soil amendments. Free catalog.

Peaceful Valley Farm Supply
P.O. Box 2209
Grass Valley, CA 95945
(916) 272-4769
(916) 272-4794 Fax

This company has long been a leader in supplying products for organic farmers, large and small, throughout the United States, including consulting services. Its large catalog includes organic fertilizers, soil amendments, seeds, bulbs, onion sets, potato seeds, grass seeds, books, and many other products. Catalog costs $2.00.

Seeds of Change
P.O. Box 15700
Santa Fe, NM 87506
(888) 762-7333

This company offers high-quality products including organic seed, organic fertilizers, soil amendments, cover crops, tools, and a wide variety of books for new and experienced gardeners, including offerings for children. Free catalog.

Further Resources

Fruit, Berry, Nut, and Garden Seed Inventory: An Inventory of Nursery Catalogs Listing All Fruit, Berry, Nut, and Garden Seed Varieties Available by Mail Order in the United States

Seed Saver Publications
Rural Route 3, Box 239
Decorah, IA 52101

A wonderful resource edited by Kent Whealy that lists varieties of fruits, nuts, and berries by name, followed by a description of color, taste, texture, growth habit, hardiness, and other relevant information, and a list of mail-order nursery sources. Also lists hundreds of vegetables by name, followed by a description of their appearance, taste, growth habit, and other relevant information, and a list of mail-order seed companies that carry seeds for them. In the front of the book is a listing of the nurseries, including their addresses and a brief description of what each nursery specializes in. Write to inquire for price and shipping charges.

Bibliography

Bailey, Liberty H. *Hortus Third: A Concise Dictionary of Plants Cultivated in the United States and Canada*. New York: Macmillan, 1976.

Brennan, Georgeanne. *Potager, Fresh Garden Cooking in the French Style*. San Francisco: Chronicle Books, 1992.

Capon, Brian. *Botany for Gardeners—An Introduction and Guide*. Portland, Oregon: Timber Press, 1990.

Larkcom, Joy. *The Salad Garden*. New York: Viking Penguin, 1990.

Puisais, Jacques, and Catherine Pierre. *Le Goût et L'Enfant*. Paris: Flammarion, 1987.

10 Easy Steps to a Young Person's Vegetable Garden. Berkeley: Division of Agricultural Sciences, University of California, November 1980.

Vilmorin-Andrieux, M.M. *The Vegetable Garden*. London: John Murray, 1885; Berkeley, California: Ten Speed Press, 1980.

Western Garden Book. Menlo Park, California: Sunset Books, 1995.

Index